The Royal United Services Institute

Defeating Complex I[n]
Beyond Iraq and Afghanistan

John Mackinlay

www.rusi.org

First Published 2005
© The Royal United Services Institute for Defence and Security Studies

All rights reserved. No part of this publication may be reproduced, stored in a retrieval system, or transmitted in any form or by any means, electronic, mechanical, photocopying, recording or otherwise, without prior permission of the Royal United Services Institute.

Whitehall Paper Series

ISBN 0-85516-117-5
ISSN 0268-1307

Series Editor: Dr Terence McNamee
Assistant Editor: Klaus Dalgaard

Whitehall Papers are available as part of a membership package, or individually at £8.00 plus p&p (£1.00 in the UK/£2.00 overseas). Orders should be sent to the Membership Administrator, RUSI Membership Office, South Park Road, Macclesfield, SK11 6SH, United Kingdom and cheques made payable to RUSI. Orders can also be made by quoting credit card details via email to: membership@rusi.org

For more details, visit our website: www.rusi.org

Printed in Great Britain by Stephen Austin & Sons Ltd. for the Royal United Services Institute, Whitehall, London, SW1A 2ET UK

RUSI is a Registered Charity (No. 210639)

Contents

Executive Summary		v
Introduction		ix
1.	**The Environment**	**1**
	Evolution of an International Response to Counter-insurgency	1
	Levels and Dimensions of the Campaign: Rise of the Virtual	8
	Significance of the Civil Population	13
2.	**Complex Insurgency**	**19**
	Frontiers of New Thinking	20
	The Cohesion Factor	24
	Defining Complex Insurgency	31
3.	**A Disunited International Response**	**40**
	Actors in the Operational Space	41
	Degrees of Coherence	45
	Manoeuvre in the Strategic Space	50
4.	**Defeating Complex Insurgency**	**53**
	Revitalize or Re-forge a more Cohesive Alliance	54
	Secure the Strategic Populations against Subversion	55
	Simplify the Operational Space	57
	Develop a New Concept of Operations	59
	Globalize the Coalition's Priorities	60
Notes		**62**

I would like to thank Hugo Slim, Alison Pargeter, Mike Shervington, Yasir Imtiaz, David Kilcullen, Victoria Wheeler, Dominick Donald and Michael Blackstad for advising me on this manuscript and my long suffering colleagues at the Royal United Services Institute for bringing it into print.

Executive Summary

Introduction
When conventional forces led by the United States attacked the Iraqi army in 1991 and 2003, their success emphasized the value of effects-based warfare and the manoeuvrist approach, especially the need to take the initiative and apply constant pressure on the enemy. However, expectations that Western military forces could exploit this approach and their technical advantages have not been realized in the campaigns to stabilize and rebuild Iraq and Afghanistan. In both cases *attrition*, rather than manoeuvre, has characterized the coalition campaign.

The central proposition of this *Whitehall Paper* is that, in addition to the short-term problems facing Coalition forces and the humanitarian/development agencies in Iraq and Afghanistan, there are fundamental reasons why the international response in both theatres cannot adopt a more manoeuvrist approach.

1. The Environment
Internationalism
At the end of the Cold War, there were three separate military cultures: the traditional peacekeepers, the continental warfighters, and, at a national level, the counter-insurgency forces. During the 1990s they were fused together to create a new identity and a new military community. This evolution imposed an international context on the counter-insurgency operations, which had become the 'bread and butter' of Coalition forces after 9/11.

Levels and Dimensions of the Campaign: Rise of the Virtual
By 2002 the Cold War definitions of conflict were eroding, a proliferation of actors now crowded into what had previously been regarded as a vertically ordered, military dominated space. This forced a reappraisal of the Cold War version of the operational level and its relationship to other levels of the conflict. The strategic and the operational remained

Executive Summary

more or less as previously defined, but a virtual dimension now surrounds, pervades and directly influences both. The virtual dimension grows in significance with the proliferation of communications; its broadcasting power and systems give a global significance to events and project them into the minds of millions in concerned populations that have operational and strategic importance.

Civil Population
In the counter-strategy against global jihad, the population is the vital ground; winning their support is a key objective for the military, the insurgents and the humanitarian actors. The relevant communities and populations are spread across the operational and strategic spaces. Within some contributing states there are minority communities which may have migrated recently into a contributor state and remain distinct from the mainstream cultures. They offer the insurgent an entry point to the strategic space.

2. Complex Insurgency

After 9/11 front line researchers seemed to agree that global insurgencies have informal structures which have adapted to, and are therefore similar to, the characteristics of the Internet. The pattern of linkages between cells is more significant than the cells themselves. Global insurgents appeared to have no centre of gravity, no globally effective leader, no hard-wired organizational structures and no single manifesto.

Although the day-to-day evidence seems to indicate a higher co-ordinating presence, the greater likelihood is that the relationship between attacks is casual and that strategic coherence is fortuitous. A complex insurgency grows organically like a virus and acts intuitively. To defeat it may require reorganized security structures and an unfamiliar modus operandi. The toughest problems in this campaign may be in a virtual dimension where the insurgency is already well established.

The spiritual dimension of global insurgency confronts the secular culture of Western analysts. To enter the mind of the subverted bomber requires understanding a faith of overwhelming intensity and a submission to God's will in the unshakeable knowledge that He will prevail.

The definition below sets out to distinguish complex insurgency from the nationally oriented forms that arose in the previous century. It also sets out to show important differences of structure and use of space, which impose a different counter-strategy.

- A complex insurgency is a campaign by globally dispersed activists and insurgents who seek to confront the culture and political ideals of a nation or group of nations that are seen to challenge their interests and way of life.
- The insurgent is assisted by the nature and energy of the virtual dimension and exploits it by growing in a networked configuration and planning kinetic actions whose images reach an audience of millions of concerned individuals.
- It is more important for globally organized insurgent forces to alter the beliefs and policies of the opposed populations than to seize territory or to overthrow a particular government with the purpose of replacing it with one representing the global movement.
- The conflict may take the form of subversion that leads to acts of terrorism. The insurgents seek to demoralize the civilian populations of the states that oppose them by threats and terrorism against their presence anywhere in the world.

3. The Disunity of the International Response

After the initial intervention, the warfighting elements of a coalition become the occupying power in a state that has ceased to function, leaving the population on the edge of survival. The insurgency therefore emerges in the context of a much wider crisis and consequently the response cannot be a narrow military affair.

The international response represents broad sectors of capability and function which are part of the overall programme for restoration. It thus comprises military coalitions, bilateral donors, the UN system, international organizations, Non-government organizations, private security companies and contractors. The media in every form will also be present at all levels, creating images and narratives for local and global audiences.

In the conflict between insurgents, host government and the international response, the complex insurgent has a number of unassailable advantages in their use of powerful messages on the theme of 'strike America', against which counter-strategy manifestos referencing the 'war on terror' fail.

The diversity of the foreign intervention causes disabling differences of approach between the sectors of the response, especially between those who do not have a shared view of the 'war on terror'. The

Executive Summary

Coalition forces and the civil actors have no key communicators, no mutual sources of policy or manifestos and no charismatic figure to unite bickering humanitarians and military forces.

Manoeuvre in the Strategic Space
The security forces have a solid warlike quality, with vertical structures and hierarchies; but their adversary has none of these and behaves, instead, like a virus growing organically, attacking instinctively and generating a virtual profile that far exceeds its real strength. The absence of moral cohesion and mutual trust prevents the international response from taking decisive action against him in the field. In addition, military commanders have no concept that allows them to move between the strategic, the tactical and the virtual with the same facility as their opponents.

In the recruitment of activists, each individual follows a linear process of: disillusionment, isolation, subversion, becoming a terrorist actor. The Coalition emphasis is on reacting to the last phase; a manoeuvrist would interrupt the first one. But the weight of our national forces is poised to react after the act of subversion has taken place, not to forestall the act itself.

4. Defeating Complex Insurgency

At present, the Coalition is incapable of achieving a more manoeuvrist – and successful – counter-strategy. To alter the balance in its favour, five key recommendations are put forward:
- Revitalize or re-forge a more cohesive alliance.
- Secure the strategic populations against subversion.
- Simplify the operational space.
- Develop a universally accepted concept of operations for international counter-insurgency operations.
- Encourage the Coalition to be more globally minded and less individually state-centred.

Introduction

The rampage of events that carried us from one strategic era to another continues. We have passed from the baleful shadow of the Cold War to grapple with a new security regime that has no name or identity, characterized above all by its complexity. Defence planners routinely face the consequences of state failure, populations at the edge of survival, humanitarian emergencies and human rights abuses on a massive scale. At the heart of these emergencies there are hostile forces, which may be globally organized and supported by the dispersed communities that provide their manpower, logistic support and moral energy. The international response is also complicated. Each facet of the crisis – security, governance, humanitarian need, human rights and economic resuscitation – requires its own sector of response.

In the prevailing security regime, these civil wars attract unmanageable international expeditionary responses. Changing values, blurred interdisciplinary boundaries and the erosion of long-standing military certainties impose a melange of actors with different values and interests on the international response. Former enemies deploy together in the same coalitions; international organizations merge to become partners in an emergency response; war and peace become indistinguishable; civilians carry guns; soldiers do humanitarian tasks; humanitarians travel in armed convoys; and peace forces deploy with battle tanks and artillery. Each contingency seems to lower the collective threshold for the use of force and involves additional sectors of expertise, a proliferation of actors and the need to accept different values and assumptions. Defence is no longer monolithic; it is not possible to understand what is happening in Afghanistan and Iraq through the restricted lenses of a military assessment. Similarly, humanitarian actors and development agencies need to understand how hostile forces also threaten their special status in the hierarchy of participants. Military training is eclectic: humanitarians, human rights officials and sundry NGOs participate in teaching and exercises. The utility of the isolated, single-discipline approach is diminishing; government departments, military staff and humanitarian actors are learning to think holistically.

John Mackinlay

Iraq and Afghanistan

During this same period of transition, after US-led coalitions achieved swift and devastating victories against Iraq's regular armed forces using smaller numbers of troops and weapons, planners became preoccupied with effects-based warfare. Commanders and staff emphasized the manoeuvrist approach, in which 'shattering the enemy's overall cohesion and will to fight, rather than his material is paramount'.[1] Defeat by disruption, by 'taking the initiative and applying constant and unacceptable pressure' became the order of the day. According to British doctrine the manoeuvrist approach calls for an attitude of mind in which doing the unexpected and seeking originality is combined with a ruthless determination to succeed. A key characteristic is to attack the enemy commander's decision-making cycle. This involves presenting him with the need to make decisions faster than he can react, so that he takes increasingly inappropriate action or none at all, thereby paralyzing his capability to fight back.[2] European and US governments began to restructure their defence forces to achieve smaller but more capable forces that could overwhelm a more numerous opponent with better technology and a superiority in 'information warfare' and 'command and control'.[3] This would enable them to seize the initiative and get inside the opposing commander's decision-making cycle by reacting faster and moving into unexpected areas of his territory.[4]

These expectations have not been realized in the post-invasion campaign to stabilize and rebuild Iraq or Afghanistan. In both cases the Coalition forces follow a reactive posture where attrition, rather than manoeuvre, has characterized their campaign. The failure of Coalition forces to get inside their adversary's decision-making cycle has been attributed to short-term tactical failures that can be rectified with time – for example, the Coalition's failure to anticipate the internal security tasks and the protracted counter-insurgency which followed their successful intervention. But these bad decisions may turn out to be tactical ephemera, the consequences of campaigning in an unfamiliar environment that will be rectified in the long term by the problem-solving energy of the US Department of Defense.

There remain, however, fundamental reasons why Coalition forces in Afghanistan and Iraq may continue to find themselves in a reactive, attritional mode even when the short-term obstacles to a more manoeuvrist approach have been removed. The larger difficulties become apparent in a holistic appraisal that reaches beyond the operational space. The relationships between the blue and red actors in the operational space can be explained crudely as an equation. The red side, the hostile forces, are informally organized and spread in a global pattern that corresponds to their supporting diaspora. Their strength is that they are hard to identify and attack; nevertheless they can demonstrate a surprising degree of ideological and practical cohesion between cells. On the blue side are the various elements of the international response – superficially they may seem to have the characteristic of a network, but there are important differences. Each element, each organization, each national contingent is largely self-dependent and arrives in the operational space with its own charter and distinct national or institutional interest. Consequently, the overwhelming characteristic of the international response is its lack of coherence and interdependence. Both the hostile forces and the response elements are organized in considerable depth beyond the operational space and respond to pressures and events beyond Afghanistan and Iraq. Both sides energetically seek the active support of the same civil populations, not just in the operational space but also beyond in the uncommitted diaspora and in the nations that provide the intervening troops and funds. Even described in these oversimplified terms, it is a complicated matrix; there is a dangerous tension between the subversive efforts of the hostile forces, the restoration and stabilizing efforts of the international response and the populations' imperative to survive on their own terms. Moreover, the triangular relationship between hostile forces, international response and concerned civil populations is reproduced on several levels beyond the operational space.

A New Strategic Era?

The central proposition of this *Whitehall Paper* is that, in addition to the short-term problems facing Coalition forces and the humanitarian/development agencies in Iraq and Afghanistan, there are fundamental reasons why the international response to global insurgency cannot adopt a more manoeuvrist approach. These include the systemic nature of the hostile forces, the characteristics of the concerned populations, the failure to recognize the different levels at which the campaign is taking place, the role of the media and the irreconcilable proliferation of actors and disciplines that comprise the international response. This paper argues that the juxtaposition of these factors and their counter-acting effect in the same operational space create an environment that is inherently unmanageable, in which it is almost impossible for the elements of the international intervention to regain the initiative from the forces that oppose them. Furthermore, that some of these greater difficulties may be the core characteristics of a strategic era rather than short-term obstacles that can be swept aside by tactical expedient.

To argue this successfully this Paper has to show that:
- Counter-insurgency takes place in an international context.
- The relationship between the actors involved is horizontal but we continue to define the conflict in vertical levels (strategic, operational and tactical) and fail to recognize the virtual dimension.
- The support and co-operation of the concerned populations is central to success. In most cases, military coalitions, insurgents and humanitarian actors are canvassing the same populations.
- The global insurgents that oppose the international coalition can be characterized as a *complex insurgency*; they grow organically and exist in considerable depth beyond the operational area. They reach and operate in every dimension of the conflict.
- To be successful, the Coalition forces, international organizations and civil agencies must act together in certain key areas.
- Coalitions tend to concentrate their effort into areas where there is least chance of achieving a manoeuvrist approach.

This Paper is organized in three parts. The first explains the environment, referring to the multinational context of counter-insurgency, the importance of civil populations and the horizontal structures that are manifested in the conflict. The second describes the adversary; the complexity of global insurgent organization; and the facility with which it can act in each dimension of the conflict. The third argues that the international response is too proliferated and disparate to conduct a manoeuvrist strategy against a complex insurgency.

1. The Environment

Evolution of an International Response to Counter-insurgency
The techniques of insurgency developed considerably during the twentieth century, but the aspirations, organization and tactics of the insurgent remained consistent with the purpose of overthrowing a particular government within the framework of a particular state. The urban Bolsheviks, the Maoists in the rural areas, Che Guevara, Carlos Marighella – in each case they sought to defeat the security forces of a national government. Consequently, during the same period, the techniques of counter-insurgency were developed in nationally different ways by each state under attack. It was a national affair, and its conduct depended greatly on the culture and values of the nation involved. Each government took an idiosyncratic view of the use of force, its own transparency, its accountability for its security forces, the freedoms of speech and of association and the status and treatment of its captured adversaries. Unlike conventional warfare, which was gradually standardized during the Cold War by the impositions of NATO and the Warsaw Pact, counter-insurgency continued to develop individually in a national idiom.

The significance of the military developments in the 1990s is that they gradually internationalized what had previously been a strictly national affair. In stark contrast to its antecedents, insurgency and its counter-strategies now have an international context, particularly in the prevailing security regime. There are disadvantages: in almost any military operation international forces are a clumsy option, and applied to the delicate civil-military processes required by successful counter-insurgency, their disadvantages become the nightmares of defeat. The purpose of this chapter, therefore, is to emphasize that counter-insurgency has an international context that has emerged with the increasing preference for the coalition force as the instrument of intervention. It is important that any consideration of a counter-strategy is continuously juxtaposed against a realistic version of the prevailing environment and the likely campaign assets arising from an international response. This section explains how international peace forces developed into coalition forces prior to 9/11 and how there has been a fusion of peace-support experience with counter-insurgency. In particular it shows how several distinct influences – the inhibitions of traditional peacekeepers, the imperatives of complex emergencies, the enduring lessons of twentieth-century counter-insurgency – are fused together in the military personality of a modern coalition. The conclusion is not that this fusion of doctrines necessarily provides us with a conceptual answer to current security challenges, for it does not. The purpose is rather to emphasize that in any post-9/11 counter-insurgency strategy, the international context is a fundamental condition. It may have the advantage of conferring greater legitimacy on the political leaders of the coalition framework, but it imposes grave tactical disadvantages on its military commanders.

Transition from a UN modus operandi
In the late 1980s, UN forces began to take action to stabilize longstanding civil emergencies and assist in the resuscitation of failing states.[1] By 1995 these actions involved more than 100,000[2] international troops, which in their authorization and command structure fell into three categories: UN peace forces; regional expeditionary forces; and military coalitions. The majority were deployed to what were referred to as complex humanitarian emergencies,[3] which arose when a number of adverse conditions were manifested together in the same space.[4] The operational space[5] for the UN's response might correspond to the territory of a host state and contain the active elements of the international force, aid agencies as well as the local military forces, civil communities and the surviving elements of the host state government. The multifunctional response comprised a diversity of humanitarian and military elements, and in terms of civil expertise and military forces usually exceeded the assets of any single agency, even the UN.

Initially, contingents approached the crisis zones[6] of the early 1990s with the same inhibitions as a traditional UN force, relying on their apparently inviolate status as peacekeepers and the consequent need to maintain consent.[7] However, by 1999 the use of bombing in Bosnia and the air-supported intervention into Kosovo by NATO coalitions showed how these inhibitions had in some cases been relaxed or abandoned, and demonstrated that a caucus of powerful nations, not the UN, now provided the military framework to take a more proactive approach. Although the body language and military capabilities of the international forces deployed in the 1990s varied considerably, military commanders had begun to accept[8] that their intent was to stabilize the environment sufficiently for the delivery of humanitarian assistance and a peace process to take place. Meanwhile, at the strategic level, the concerned states involved in brokering peace agreements failed to acknowledge[9] that a successful peace process often confronted interests of indigenous armed factions. In particular it deprived faction leaders of their local power, sources of enormous wealth and exposed some to retribution in the international courts; therefore, in many cases they resisted.

Containment Operations by Coalition Forces
After Dayton, the mobilization of NATO forces to guarantee a peace process seemed to emphasize the diminution of the UN's status as a global convenor of international peace forces. Generically, coalition forces now exercised a warfighting capability and a determination to use it if necessary in order to establish a presence in the host state. However, once established they displayed less determination to continue the intensive and controversial procedures needed to restore a monopoly of military power into the hands of a new state government. Instead, the military control of the operational space would normally be ceded to a civil administration. The latter's priorities lay in civil and humanitarian concerns rather than crushing or neutralizing the rump of a continued opposition. Nevertheless, despite the palpable presence of disaffected and armed elements of local populations, coalition forces generally operated at a level of commitment that indicated a containment posture.[10] Consequently, where the operational areas remained insecure, local families and individuals were left unprotected and foreign assistance was lost or degraded by extortion and looting. In addition, armed factions could interdict humanitarian relief convoys and commit crimes, thereby exposing the peace process to manipulation.

By the time Kosovo had been stabilized, an increasingly familiar operational process, now referred to as containment, drew together the principal actors of an emerging culture of military intervention, based largely on the NATO experience in the Balkans. This process can be identified as having two or three operational phases[11] that occurred between the arrival of a military intervention force and its reaching a plateau of activity that indicated the start of a garrison phase.

John Mackinlay

Moving from Containment to Intervention

Meanwhile, during the 1990s, as international forces of various kinds continued to deploy to complex humanitarian emergencies, the nature of insurgency had mutated. In poor and insecure countries, which were sometimes the epicentres of complex emergencies, global changes had altered the relationship between a failing government and the forces that sought to overthrow them. This was particularly the case in those failed states categorized as black holes[12] in the international structure, where a continuous state of anarchy discouraged any serious restoration efforts by the international community. It can be argued that the policy of containment, which merely dampened the effects of a complex humanitarian emergency without taking military action to restore a monopoly of violence, had favoured internationally organized forms of insurgency that needed an unclaimed, un-policed space in which to establish themselves.[13]

The attacks on the US on 11 September 2001 diminished the significance of Kosovo and the containment model as a milestone in our doctrinal development. In their response to 9/11, the US went beyond containment and moved the 'intervention community', if such a thing had ever really existed, across the threshold of a new chapter of operations. The 9/11 attack served to reduce, or remove altogether, the perception of distance as a safety curtain between the rich, safe countries (which habitually responded to complex emergencies) and the hostile forces that opposed them in the faraway black holes. The Bosnia-Kosovo response model was jeopardized by this development; containment could not be considered as an effective measure. A globally organized insurgent force, based in a black hole state or a poorly contained area, had demonstrated the capability of mounting a devastating attack on the most protected cities in the US and Western nations. This increased Western resolve to contribute armed forces in a more committed and interventionist way towards a collective solution.

Historically, alliances take time to mature and absorb the capricious behaviour of individual members as well as respond to military contingencies.[14] The prototype version of a counter-strategy in Afghanistan was more complicated than previous coalitions and involved many sectors of the US government in an operation that was multidimensional as well as international. Understandably, the Afghanistan and Iraq interventions developed in an ad hoc manner, initially following the familiar routines of containment. However, in the first few months after the arrival of the military forces, several events and characteristics distinguished what happened in Afghanistan from the 1990s or even the Kosovo model of containment. In particular, two differently constituted military forces, with separate tactical missions, co-existed in the same space: the UN-authorized International Security Assistance Force maintaining security in the Kabul urban areas and, under a separate command authority, the mainly US troops campaigning to destroy Taliban and Al-Qa'ida in a wider area that extended over the North West Frontier Provinces of Pakistan and northward into Kashmir. In the stabilizing phase, its main aim was not just to contain the opposing forces, but to destroy them and dismantle their organization. To achieve this, the campaigning element comprised a much greater proportion of combat troops, combat aircraft, armour and artillery than the preceding expeditions. Thus, in political terms, 9/11 forced the US and its Coalition partners across a threshold from containment to intervention. At the strategic level, the importance of the UN as mandating authority has been further diminished. As expeditionary military capability increased, the centre of gravity for organizing and commanding international forces moved first of all from New York to Brussels and after 9/11 to US CENTCOM in Tampa, Florida. The large conscript armies of NATO and former Warsaw Pact countries had downsized as a consequence of the Cold War, but almost immediately the complexity and recurring demands of participating in international forces has imposed a further round of reorganization and re-evaluation of defence priorities and capabilities.

At the operational level, the soldiers on the ground found themselves in an environment which continued to grow increasingly complicated. Previously, the peacekeepers' operational space had been an empty desert between two inert armies; now it was crowded with independent actors, most of whom had an equally important role in the success of the peace process. New actors brought new sectors of competence to the operational space, and in some cases longstanding participants found themselves supplanted by contractors and private military companies. The operational space also continued to grow more dangerous. The local militias and bandit gangs who challenged peace processes in the mid-90s had been less potent than the internationally organized insurgents that indiscriminately attacked all who were associated with the rebuilding process both within and beyond the operational space.

A Fusion of Cultures
At the end of the Cold War there were three separate military cultures: the traditional peacekeepers, the continental warfighters and, at a national

level, the counter-insurgency forces. Each culture had its own clique of military commanders, support industries, research academics and communicators. During the Cold War the US and Russians dominated the mass warfighting culture; the international peacekeepers were led by the Nordic nations and the Canadians. Counter-insurgency developed nationally, the expertise lay in individual armies such as the British, French and the US, but also with states such as South Africa, Israel and Rhodesia, which gave it a strongly negative connotation.

During the 1990s the trend of operations compelled defence forces to review and alter their doctrine. Simultaneously, the three distinct military cultures which grew out of the contingencies of the Cold War period were de facto fusing together to create a new identity. The peacekeeping culture survived, and after improving its military planning capability the Department of Peacekeeping Operations (DPKO) in UN HQ New York continued its global supervision of observers and peace forces. The UN continues to deploy what are, in effect, containment forces, and this has brought the level of UN-led forces in the field to approximately 65,000 troops in 2005. Counter-insurgency metamorphosed into the new peace forces in the form of doctrine and tactical techniques, and nationally efforts were made to share training and doctrinal information. In this way, elements of counter-insurgency experience survived, both in the form of institutional wisdom and doctrine.[15] The mass warfighters provided new participating nations from both sides of the former East-West divide. Staff from East and West European countries deployed under NATO to direct stabilization operations; new planning cells were established to cope with doctrine development, crisis response and civil-military co-operation. The international force was acquiring an identity and a greater importance as a nucleus that borrowed elements from three previous military cultures. The number of regular national contributors rose to seventy in 1995, and by 2004 comprised more than a hundred states. International forces were generally directed at the highest level by a civil appointee who had the wider task of pulling together the array of civil and military assets that comprise the international response, ostensibly to represent their collective political authority but also to co-ordinate their actions.

The evolutionary process had a linear appearance (traditional peacekeeping, followed by containment, followed by intervention), but in reality the three forms co-existed simultaneously. The chart[16] below shows the approximate relationship of these separate categories in terms of their scale and the relative numbers of deployed troops.

Category of Force	Location	Total Troops
Intervention Forces	Afghanistan	11,000
	Iraq	170,000
		(181,000)
Containment Forces (NATO / EU)	Bosnia	12,000
	Kosovo	23,000
	Kabul (ISAF)	6,500
		(41,500)
Containment Forces (UN)	Sierra Leone	11,539
	DRC	10,576
	Liberia	14,833
	Côte d'Ivoire	3,036
	Burundi	5.650
		(45,634)
Traditional Peacekeeping Forces and Observers	Middle Eastern Region UNTSO	153
	India / Pakistan border	44
	Cyprus	1202
	Golan	1029
	South Lebanon	1994
	Western Sahara	230
	Georgia	118
	Kosovo	36
	Ethiopia / Eritrea	4006
	Haiti	240
	East Timor	1609
		(10,661)

In this way, a new military community and culture emerged after the end of the Cold War that was less defined, more facetted and more complicated than previous expeditionary formations. It grew from three elements: the new wave of more powerful contingents and their equipment came from the warfighting culture; the appearance, the language and some of the procedures of international organizations came from the traditional peacekeepers; and from counter-insurgency came the adoption of a modus operandi, ostensibly from a previous operational era, but nevertheless with important practical relevance to the resuscitation of the state and its security organs.

At a political level, a nucleus of contingent providers was increasingly identified by their common political outlook, doctrines, organizations and procedures, some of which had emerged during the Cold War. However, the international context of counter-insurgency in a coalition force has grave military disadvantages. Each contingent is conditioned by its own cultural values and national approach. This imposes discord and disunity on the campaign. In the Iraqi operational space there has already been a variety of responses on key issues such as freedom of access to the media, accountability of military forces in terms of civil law and differences in the treatment of captured adversaries and techniques of interrogation.

Levels and Dimensions of the Campaign: Rise of the Virtual

Doctrine writers tend to define conflict as taking place at different levels. For example, British doctrine describes the Gulf War in terms of the grand strategic, the military strategic, the operational and the tactical levels.[17] However, by 1995 the Cold War definitions of a war zone were eroding; new challenges and a proliferation of actors now crowded into what had previously been regarded as a military dominated space, and military thinkers, particularly at Western defence colleges, began to address the altering environment of complex emergencies.[18] In addition to the multinational force, the operational space now contained an array of civil actors who were also essential to the overall success of the campaign. Like the military, each civil agency had a higher level of command that lay beyond the operational space. Cold War doctrine on the levels of war was also confronted by the pervasive presence of local, national and international news networks in the operational space, which had the effect of compressing the traditional version (strategic, operational and tactical) of different campaign levels into a single entity. Communications technology could transmit images of an incident involving a few soldiers in a remote place simultaneously to every level of the concerned international community. By 2004, the UK Ministry of Defence was emphasizing that 'the comments and actions of a corporal may prompt ministerial statements as a result of media reporting'.[19] Furthermore, the 'strategic corporal' phenomenon might lead senior commanders and ministers at the highest level to interfere in a corporal's decisions to prevent damaging mistakes at the lowest level.[20] In this way the proliferation of actors in the operational space, as well as remarkable advances in communications technology, had altered the environment for international force operations.

After 9/11 the more palpable threat of globally organized insurgents moved coalition forces – and, de facto, the civil elements of the response, too – into the more adversarial environment of a proxy war zone. Calling it a 'proxy war zone' recognized another set of actors in the operational space – the array of adversaries, differently constituted and motivated but nevertheless connected to each other and their sustaining populations by an informal network of extremely modern communication systems. This development forced us to rethink the Cold War version in which the operational space was deemed to have a vertical relationship to other levels of the conflict. In the emerging approach, the strategic and operational levels correspond approximately to the definitions that remain in current doctrine.[21] Although the 2004 British doctrine recognized the phenomenon of 'compression',[22] it failed to recognize a *virtual dimension*, which seemed to be the main factor driving this development. A more complete description of the dimensions (rather than levels) of this particular type of conflict would include the strategic and the operational, more or less as previously defined, but without separating them from the virtual dimension that encloses and directly influences both. The purpose of this section, therefore, is to describe the operational, strategic and the virtual in the context of a complex insurgency and its counter-strategy.

The Operational Space
In contrast to the strategic and virtual, the operational space is to a large extent a palpable area of terra firma. In the context of an intervention it usually encloses the host state and its capital city, which are at the epicentre of the crisis. However, the edges of the operational space may extend beyond the boundaries of the host state to include populations divided by arbitrarily drawn borders. The ports, airheads and regional entry points used by the international response are also regarded as being part of the operational space.[23] In a less tangible sense, the boundaries between the operational and the strategic are now blurred by the increased amount of interaction between ministries, governments and humanitarian actors. Although this happens beyond the physical margins of the operational space, these activities are operational in their substance and consequences.

Therefore, in addition to the host state, the operational terra firma and its adjoining sea areas are occupied by the international military forces, the humanitarian actors,[24] the remaining elements of the civil response,[25] the flat-pack versions of the contributor states' embassies,[26] representative

HQ and staff of the major international organizations and, most significantly, the array of different adversaries who oppose the international response. In the context of an intervention, therefore, the operational space is a proxy war zone, in contrast to that of a containment operation, where there is a much greater degree of neutral territory. In an intervention, the actions of the internationally organized insurgent groups against their declared target list, which includes the host government and the humanitarian actors, reduces or entirely removes the possibility of exploiting 'humanitarian space',[27] so that the opportunities for even a small and intrepid NGO to work in this potentially hostile territory are greatly reduced. In exceptional cases it is possible for an organization of global standing to negotiate a neutral status for itself, but the majority of the international response works and lives within an envelope of security that is provided by the host state or the leaders of the coalition. Consequently, many of the non-military rebuilding tasks are delegated to commercial companies and private security companies (PSCs) rather than NGOs, in contrast to a less contested operational space where the objective is to contain rather than to intervene. The edge of the coalition's security envelope implies that beyond it there are no-go areas that are routinely contested by insurgents or held by warlords whose support for the rebuilding process is fickle and conditioned by personal interests. The operational space of what is in effect a proxy war[28] zone is therefore defined by the combination of international actors, the international insurgents that oppose them and the intensity of hostilities throughout the area.

Strategic Space
When an intervention is challenged by a globally organized insurgency, and the operational space is therefore a proxy war zone, the related strategic space refers to a global area in which the parties in contest have interests and resources. Where a coalition force is threatened by insurgent forces inspired by Islamic radical activism, the strategic space may include the sixty or so cities identified by the CIA as having a significant Muslim migrant community, situated as far north as Stockholm and as far south as Sydney. It may also include the airspace and sea areas used by the warfighting elements of the international forces that are far removed from the related operational space. In a less territorial sense, the strategic space is also identified by actors and institutions that have a relationship to the operation. These include states with significant migrant or indigenous populations that are politically or ideologically interested in the conflict

and states which are contributing troops, assets and cash to the international response. The strategic space also encloses the HQs of global, regional and international organizations that have a role in the conflict. The reactions of an international forum may impact directly on the success and failure of the campaign in the form of a gridlocked UN Security Council, an antagonistic UN General Assembly or a hotly divided EU. They seem to be far away from the dust and heat of the conflict, but their rhetoric and actions impact directly on the unity and resolve of the actors at the operational level. They are, therefore, strategically linked to the success and safety of the corporal leading his patrol on the streets of Kabul or Baghdad.

A counter-strategy against a globally organized insurgent force also requires being global in its scope. If the insurgent is recruited, armed, financed, motivated and deployed by different cells of a network that is spread across the world, the elements of the counter-strategy must be correspondingly spread as well as integrated in each city and population where it seeks to take offensive action. Again, this raises the question of boundaries between the strategic and operational, but in a different sense to that of the 'compression' involving the 'strategic corporal'. The geographically separate and nationally distinct counter-operations in London, Jakarta and Karachi, for example, become increasingly merged together, blurring the boundaries between national operations and operations within a particular war zone such as Iraq – especially when they are all directed towards the same hostile organization. The strategic level, defined with Churchillian certainty by Cold War doctrine writers, is therefore being eroded by the horizontal spread of our opponents and the similarly spreading echelons of the counter-strategy.

The vertical structures that previously defined conflict for military thinkers (strategic, operational and tactical) must be adapted to the array of actors involved within them and to the horizontal nature of networks that have no apparent hierarchy. The multinational elements are conceptually anchored in this respect by their own institutional nature and that of the lead nations and global organizations (UN, ICRC, World Bank, etc.). The latter have an essential role to play but they impose a hierarchical approach on the response. But on the opposing side, the insurgents are informally organized, global in their reach and can act with great facility at the operational and strategic levels.

The Virtual Dimension
Whereas the strategic and the operational refer largely to events and activities that have a physical nature, virtual activities (as later defined) may produce an effect that is not immediately palpable in terms of ships sunk and territory seized. The consequences of virtual action are measured by opinion polls, election results, altered markets, sometimes by riots on the street and later by the measure of popular assistance and support for a peace process or an insurgent organization. Strategic and operational activities generally present themselves in places and spaces that exist in a physical sense, but the virtual war zone is the human mind. In this sense the virtual is substantially different to the physical character of the strategic and operational. This dissimilarity compels the traditionalist doctrine writer to resist its consideration as 'a level of war'. But faced with a horizontally ordered conflict zone, we have to move beyond the conventional, think laterally and, if necessary, include a virtual dimension that recognizes an overwhelming relationship between what happens in the human mind and what happens in the strategic and operational spaces; this may require us to abandon a vertical interpretation of conflict.

The virtual dimension is important wherever communities that are relevant to the conflict exist. At the front lines it includes the soldiers who comprise the intervening coalition force as well as the insurgents who oppose them. The nations and populations which support the coalition and its associated nation-building efforts are also part of the virtual dimension of activity, as are the concerned Muslim migrant communities across the world that either support or oppose the insurgent. The virtual dimension refers, therefore, to the entire process of image making, news gathering and their promulgation, which alters, weakens or reinforces the beliefs of the concerned populations.

The virtual dimension grows in significance with the proliferation of communications. On 7 July 2005 the atrocity by the London bombers took place – with the exception of the bomb exploded on the number 30 bus – in the obscurity of several deep tunnels, hundreds of feet below the ground. Despite the absence of the international press corps, within a few hours this event was translated into many languages and projected worldwide into the minds of millions of listeners and viewers to become an act with massive consequences for Britain's multiracial society and its foreign policy in Iraq. It was a dramatic atrocity; but the broadcasting power of the actors and systems in the virtual dimension gave it global visibility and projected it into millions of minds with immediate operational and strategic consequences.

In this example, the processes in the virtual dimension fall into two groups:[29]

- The commercial news services, regarded as the regulated element of the virtual dimension, quickly create versions of the event which are sold, resold and disseminated to become the vision, sound and print icons of the atrocity.
- The unregulated element, referred to as the 'viral' actors, in the virtual dimension creates parallel but less authoritative versions of the same event. The mobile phone is usually the initial information source, and by connecting the phone user to individual websites or bloggers, this version gets rapidly disseminated on a lesser scale.

The viral version is in many cases linked back to the regulated commercial version by reporters in every region of the world trawling websites for immediate news of the event. Consequently, the political and emotional potential of the event is realized by the different systems in the virtual dimension and not by the physical circumstances of the attack itself.

Until recently, 'information warfare' has been regarded as a technique, part of a range of techniques including 'command and control warfare' that are available to a military commander. The virtual dimension should not be confused with information warfare and must be regarded as an arena of activity that no single party controls; it is not, therefore, a special weapon exclusively in the hands of any particular user. Just as friendly and enemy forces act against each other in the strategic and operational spaces, so they do in the virtual dimension. The consequences of their actions in one space impact in the others, reducing the separations between the operational, the strategic and the virtual. In this manner, a proliferation of actors and systems in the virtual dimension has created a theatre of war with key objectives and tactically significant areas that can be seized by either side. Later this paper will show that globally organized insurgents move with great facility and effect between the strategic, the operational and the virtual. To defeat them requires:

- First, a recognition of the characteristics of complex insurgency; and
- Second, that a counter-strategy has operational, strategic and virtual dimensions, which are strongly interconnected.

Significance of the Civil Population

A number of senior officials returning from Iraq and Afghanistan in 2005 have pointed out the significance of the population in the Coalition's campaign to stabilize the operational space. A particular general said famously at a meeting in Norfolk, Virginia, 'the local population is the vital ground'.[30] This apparently simplistic observation deserves greater scrutiny, for its interpretation has many consequences for both complex insurgency and the counter-strategy.

In Cold War parlance the 'vital ground' was a tactical expression that referred to an actual piece of ground on the battlefield that was central to winning or losing in the short term. By gaining it the attacker was certain to take the position, just as by losing it the defender would ultimately be driven off. In the context of Iraq or Afghanistan, however, winning the vital ground refers to the support of the population and raises key questions, such as:

- Which populations comprise the vital ground, the local populations in the operational space or the 'strategic populations' further afield?
- What role does a population play and how does it relate to the actors in the operational space?
- Whose vital ground is it? (In addition to the military, the insurgents and the humanitarian actors also have reasons to regard populations as their primary objectives.)

Which Population?

Although the observation from the Norfolk conference referred to a 'local population', there are many additional categories of community and population which are relevant to international intervention and the resistance to it. In the operational space there are different elements of the host population, which in Afghanistan and Iraq is divided by ethnicity and religion. In military terms, each element of the host population is essential to success. Winning their support for the stabilization and reconstruction process is a 'vital' objective. However, immediately beyond the political borders of the host state there are other populations, which also impact directly on the success or failure of the insurgency. In Afghanistan, these influences might lie in Pakistan, Tajikistan, Uzbekistan and Iran. In Iraq, they might lie in Turkey, Syria and again in Iran.

Beyond the operational space there are also strategically significant populations whose support or disaffection impact directly on the campaign as well. In a contributing state such as the US or UK, these populations can be broadly classified as the cultural majority by which a nation is identified. Within the same states are much smaller minority communities which may have migrated recently into a contributor state and remain distinct from the mainstream cultures. The figures that would explain the relative size of a migrant community and its relationship to the majority population are imprecise,[31] and this vagueness is compounded by the illegally immigrated element. Each majority population assimilates minority communities with different degrees of success.[32]

The Roles of Different Populations in the Campaign
Different populations exercise varying influences on the success of the counter-strategy. The support of the strategic population, particularly the political majority of a contributor state, is essential to the continuation of the military campaign. A visible and effective protest movement against military intervention has the effect of demoralizing troops on the ground and may in due course persuade national media and local politicians to join the anti-war movement. Once the protest gains momentum and visibility, it becomes self-sustaining and may override democratic and parliamentary authority. In British doctrine, a coalition's cohesion is regarded as its centre of gravity,[33] and the supportive attitude of the population of each contributor state is crucial to maintaining that cohesion.

Concerned immigrant minorities (described above) may live in a contributor state or in a state not connected to the conflict. In a global insurgency that is energized by Muslim radical activism, their relevance to the conflict may be that they are a Muslim community in which there is concern about the circumstances in the distant operational space. This concern may be exploited by individuals connected to the global insurgency. If members can be subverted to provide active support for insurgents, the community itself takes on a significance that far outweighs its comparatively small numbers. The subverted elements become part of a wider network that has the potential to provide refuge, manpower and logistic support to the insurgent forces.

In the operational space, the host population has a more direct significance to the progress of the campaign. Generally, a coalition commander is seeking to restore a degree of security that would allow the population to return to its commercial and social routines. The insurgent force strives to prevent this. Both sides need the support of the population to achieve their aims. The coalition commander continuously persuades the population to risk the hazard of taking to the streets to restart the heartbeat of the local area and to assist his security measures by denying the insurgent support. The coalition's relationship towards the population, as a result, becomes conditional: 'give me your support and I will give you my resources.'[34] The population are at the tipping-point of the campaign. If they decide to support the coalition forces, the counter-strategy begins to take effect and gain momentum; the insurgents will become increasingly cut off from their sources of support, boxed in by poor intelligence and an unsympathetic environment. However, if the coalition fails to win the population, they are themselves in a hostile environment and without intelligence. Winning the support of the host population is therefore a key military objective in the operational space.

Whose Vital Ground?
In a conventional conflict for territory the vital ground is inanimate, and both the enemy and friendly forces wish to hold it for similar reasons. In this context, the populations identified as the vital ground are volatile, take many forms, are spread across the tactical and strategic spaces and their support is essential to several different parties. The chief contestants for the support of this array of concerned populations are the coalition states, the insurgents who oppose them and the humanitarian actors. As explained above, the coalition states need the support of the strategic population, and above all their own constituent populations, in order to maintain the coherence of the intervention force. They also need to win the loyalty of the concerned immigrant minorities within their constituencies, which may otherwise be subverted by the insurgents. Failure to do this threatens homeland security and has, in the case of Spain, led to an atrocity that directly caused the withdrawal of Spain's contingent from the coalition. The coalition forces in the operational area also seek the support of the host-state population for different reasons as explained above.

The insurgents seek to mobilize the same populations, but in the opposing direction. They achieve this in different ways. Against the majority of the indigenous populations of contributor states, they use the techniques of terrorism, and their attacks are amplified and carried into the minds of a huge target audience for them by the energy of the virtual dimension. Towards the immigrant minorities, who may share the same ideology as themselves, they use the tactics of persuasion, taking advantage of the prolific communication networks in the virtual dimension. In the operational space, their tipping factor is also the support of the host population, whom they must persuade or coerce into rejecting the stabilizing efforts of the intervention and the associated development programmes.

The multi-mandated development agencies also target the same populations but in quite a different way to the coalition force and the insurgents. Non-government organizations, in particular, need to maintain a high level of public concern for the situation in the operational space if they are to sustain their own funding. Although anxious to distance themselves from all forms of military life,[35] they nevertheless stand to lose government funds and operational security in the event of a political change of direction against the military intervention within a contributor state. In many cases they are caught between their inherently anti-war perspective and the need to respond alongside a larger international intervention which is also military. In the operational space, the humanitarian programme does not have a tipping-point in the same manner as a military campaign. The humanitarian concerns are to reach and assist the elements of the population which are suffering or at risk 'in accordance with the overriding core principles of humanity, neutrality and impartiality.'[36] However, their imperative to establish a neutral access to the host population brings them into confrontation with the insurgents and the coalition forces that both need to capture the support of the same population, but on their own terms.

In the previous century, Mao, the great exponent of 'people's war', and Robert Thompson, the architect of an effective counter-strategy, both understood the importance of the population in the context of insurgency. However, as insurgency begins to assume a complex, networked characteristic, the issue of popular support also becomes commensurately complicated. The horizontally ordered conflict area explained in the previous section prompts wider questions about communities beyond the operational space, whose support is essential both to the insurgent and to a successful counter-strategy. For different reasons, the humanitarian actors, the insurgents and the coalition forces urgently seek to establish a relationship with the same concerned populations. Their objectives are mutually exclusive; this is not surprising to the insurgents, but it is a source of continuous surprise and rivalry for the civil agencies and the military, which ostensibly emanate from the same culture, the same contributor populations and are part of the same international initiatives.[37]

*

The response to 9/11 and the mass of analysis that followed, demonstrated that we are in a security era of interventions led and dominated by US forces that are opposed by insurgents who are globally organized. The environment of insurgency and counter-insurgency has been altered by global changes, meanwhile military doctrine in this respect has stood still, and there has been no articulation of a counter-strategy in the context of a post-9/11 environment. The history of insurgency shows that a successful counter-strategy is holistic, but achieving holism in these changed circumstances compels the doctrine writer to venture into an unfamiliar landscape, include strange partners and embrace new disciplines. New thinking may even require the US military imperative for a purely US response be subordinated to the political advantages of a more globally representative coalition force. It now has to be a planning assumption that any future counter-strategy against a global insurgency will be international and that the well-known military disadvantages of this are constant factors in any campaign. New thinking also requires a revised version of the levels of war that recognizes the horizontal nature of the actors involved. The virtual dimension of conflict has to become an integral part of every plan, not a specialist area for 'spin' experts and network geeks who are regarded with suspicion and habitually excluded from the operational heart of every military HQ. The human mind is a theatre of war; it has its own landscape of vital objectives, which have to be linked to strategic and operational actions. A new doctrine will also have to rationalize the tangled landscape of different populations that sustain the conflict either by supporting the international coalition or the forces that oppose it; they constitute the vital ground of future campaigns. This incomplete description conveys some operational characteristics of the prevailing era. A realistic proposal for a counter-strategy has to be set in this context.

2. Complex Insurgency

In conventional war, staff officers were taught to consider the ground before the enemy. This allowed them to assess the relationship of hostile weapons and troops to a landscape where the advantages and disadvantages of each feature were already understood. Similarly, in a global insurgency the ground, or in this case the environment, has important characteristics that impinge on the forces and agencies involved and, furthermore, distinguish it from pre-9/11 versions of counter-strategy. These features, described in Chapter One, included the horizontal relationships between actors, the consequent fusion of the levels of war and the importance of the virtual dimension and its networked characteristics.

Research writers reacted to the post-9/11 environment by describing it as a new security paradigm in which the characteristics of the adversary have gradually emerged. The global insurgent is an extremely modern phenomenon, a virus that has exploited global change, thrived in a networked environment and swiftly adapted to each new chapter of technical development, especially in the transfer and propagation of information. However, in this mass of new writing there are important contradictions, particularly arising from the insurgents' apparent lack of structures versus their ability to organize worldwide. Several recent observers characterize the insurgents as leaderless, unstructured groups that are haphazardly strung together across the strategic and operational space in a configuration that is similar to the Internet. Yet this casually formed, leaderless network has shown itself capable on several occasions of co-ordinating sophisticated attacks, which impact on strategic populations as well as the day-to-day security of the operational area. Despite the apparent absence of an organizational structure there is a powerful cohesive factor at work, which causes the separated nodes of the insurgent group to act in what appears to be a highly concerted manner. If what we describe as a global insurgency was a deliberative organization, created cell-by-cell, block-by-block, by Osama bin Laden acting in the manner of a revolutionary leader, it would be easier to understand. The reality is that the globally dispersed insurgency, which we now see with greater clarity, grew by itself. It operates in the manner that it grew, bottom-up, by exploiting opportunities that arise naturally. Its complexity arises from the different forces and characteristics, which give each group within this constellation the ability to survive and operate successfully.

This chapter sets out to provide a generic explanation of what is meant by complex insurgency. It analyzes the most recent research writing on the current jihadist insurgency, in particular three papers, which separately come to similar conclusions about the way insurgent forces have grown and organized themselves and the influence of the Internet on these developments. It sets out to resolve the paradox of how these apparently disparate groups manage, nevertheless, to act in a mutually reinforcing manner so that an attack on a strategic target reverberates with such effect in the operational space and in the virtual dimension. Several writers explain the cohesion factor to some extent as the significance of faith. With the benefit of analysis spanning its temporal and spiritual characteristics, the final section of this chapter defines complex insurgency and explains why our adversaries are able to act with such facility in each space or dimension of the conflict.

Frontiers of New Thinking

In the 1990s John Arquilla and David Ronfeldt explained the significance of network-based conflict, claiming that it would become a major phenomenon in the decades ahead.[1] They distinguished Net war from the activities of hackers and the science-fiction propositions for linking computer aggression to stand-off attacks on cyberspace. Rather than bringing the Internet 'down', Arquilla and Rondfeldt insisted (in their updated thesis)[2] that genuine Net warriors have a vested interest in keeping the Net 'up' because they 'benefit from using the Internet and other advanced communications services for purposes that range from co-ordinating with each other and seeking recruits, to projecting their identity, broadcasting their messages to target audiences, and gathering intelligence about their opponents'.[3] Arquilla and Rondfeldt's descriptions of the technical characteristics of the Internet seemed to mirror the organization of the insurgents who were using it so successfully. The 'chains', 'hubs' and 'all channel networks' which allowed traffic to pass in any direction, between individuals and from an individual to a multitude of recipients, resonated with the informality and energy of the insurgent groups that were increasingly using it. Moreover, the enormous proliferation of systems makes it hard to prevent this traffic from reaching an audience. Arquilla and Rodfeldt concluded that a structured hierarchy would have a difficult time fighting networks because of the robust and survivable nature of a casually expanding system and also because the vertical, deliberative nature of the opposing coalition is antithetical to a horizontally growing Net. In the recent past, determined groups had demonstrated this by defying government counter-measures against their Internet campaigns in Algeria and Mexico.[4] In Arquilla and Rodfeldt's estimation, it required a network to fight a network; moreover, to do this successfully, the vertical hierarchies associated with the government side would have to 'innovate organisationally and doctrinally'. Whichever side mastered the network first gained major advantages in terms of network intuition that would enable it to survive by innovation and keeping ahead of its less acclimatized adversary. Although Arquilla and Rodfeldt's direct and practical approach successfully demystified Net war, they wrote from the perspectives of Net experts. The obvious next step would have been to incorporate their conclusions into a wider counter-strategy. But few nations seem to have the vision or the facilities to link an information counter-offensive on the network to a military campaign, particularly in an international environment.[5]

Writing from a more military perspective in June 2004, Bruce Hoffman saw Iraq as a counter-insurgency campaign, despite the prevailing academic trend for explaining low-level violence as terrorism. Hoffman assessed US military actions against principles of counter-insurgency doctrine that had been established by the British and US forces in previous campaigns. Resisting General Abizaid's description of Iraq as a classical counter-guerrilla campaign, Hoffman insisted that the insurgents have no centre of gravity, no leader, no hard-wired organizational structures and no single manifesto. Their flat, lineal networks conformed to Arquilla and Rodfeldt's Net war rather than the pyramid shapes of conventional forces. He concluded that our national counter-strategies may be irrelevant and that coalition governments will have to adapt themselves to the unusual characteristics of a global opponent. The interest of Hoffman's description of the informal, horizontal character of the insurgency in Iraq is that these characteristics correspond to the Internet, which played such an important part in their success.

More recently, David Kilcullen, in a separate research paper,[6] has expanded Hoffman's conclusions about the campaign and the military manifestations of Net war. Killculen also convincingly demolishes the academic fashion for interpreting global insurgency as terrorism.[7] According to him, wrong definitions of terrorism originated from the 1970s studies of 'international terrorism' that referred to disembodied groups, including Bader-Meinhoff, Italy's Red Brigades and Japan's Red Army. This terrorist paradigm has been continuously confused with that of insurgent groups that are more pervasively established, but who are nevertheless wrongly described as terrorists, presumably because they use acts of terror as a tactical option. Wrong definitions lead to wrong counter-strategies; counter-terrorism implies reactive short-term measures associated with close protection specialists, police and low-level human intelligence. Whereas in the more authoritative doctrine, counter-insurgency[8] is a long-term campaign that is politically determined and involves the leaders of civil society, in addition to the police and military that are associated with counter-terrorism. It is possible to argue that the wrong naming of the 'war on terror' has retarded the formulation of an effective counter-strategy by several years.

Kilcullen charts an array of distinct jihadist insurgent campaigns from North Africa to South Asia,[9] and shows how common interests and a developed exploitation of the Internet have linked them together. Although in each insurgent theatre the local grievances and actors are not directly associated with the objectives of global jihad, it is the linkages between theatres which are critical to the wider success of the global movement. In a technical sense the rash of insurgent cells are manifestations of the Internet, but at a deeper level they are the product of shared ideologies, culture, history and family connections. Like Hoffman, he argues that traditional counter-insurgency doctrine derived from national experience cannot address the complexity or the international spread of actors associated with countering global insurgents connected by the Internet.

Kilcullen assumes that no world government will emerge with sufficient authority or power to run an integrated counter-insurgency campaign to isolate the adversary from its system of mutual support. Without a single 'co-ordinating Supremo', a concept of a global counter-strategy that merely extrapolates from national experience, or a global version of traditional counter-insurgency, cannot, in his view, succeed. Kilcullens's counter-proposal is described as a strategy of disaggregation, which would seek to interdict 'the links between theatres, denying the ability of regional and global actors to link and exploit local actors, disrupting flows between and within jihad theatres'.[10]

In February 2005, a restricted version of a draft prepared for OSD and published by RAND[11] reinforced many of the conclusions reached independently by individuals cited above.[12] The RAND team (Brennan, Grissom, Daly, Chalk, Rosenau, Sepp and Dalzell), like Hoffman and Kilcullen, also took the view that Al-Qa'ida should be regarded as 'the first truly global insurgency', and that to avoid further conceptual confusion, analysts were enjoined to use the US State Department's definition[13] of terrorism and the CIA's definition of insurgency rather than that of the US Department of Defence.[14] The RAND study sets out to show how insurgencies have changed over time and to analyze 'the construct of a networked insurgency'. Like Kilcullen, RAND emphasize the critical importance of the relationship between the nodes of the insurgent network. This development led them to conclude that prevailing insurgencies, particularly in the array of theatres indicated by Kicullen above, are increasingly federated to each other and to other organizations and groups across traditional boundaries that were imposed by differences of interest and ethnicity. This, for example, has encouraged criminal gangs to work alongside insurgents and jihadists to form what RAND called a Federated Insurgency Complex (FIC). An FIC takes the form of a multiplex network with a hub-core-periphery relationship that mirrored the characteristics of the Internet. Like Hoffman and Kilcullen, RAND believed that the 'standard counter insurgency tactics' of the twentieth century could not defeat an FIC whose sparse linkages and informal organization make it a poor target for conventional forces using a 'find, fix and track' methodology.[15] Nevertheless, the RAND study suggests that FICs are vulnerable because their continued growth and coherence relies on mutual trust between nodes, and individually, these have a propensity for factionalism. The study concludes that a new strategy is required, which relies on the participation of other US government departments.[16] In common with the previous papers, the RAND study also concludes that the US Department of Defense programme for transformation and its reliance on manoeuvre operations are more relevant to the contingencies of the twentieth century than the destruction of FICs. Moreover, US military doctrine for counter-insurgency was similarly backward-looking and more appropriate to Maoist insurgency than a globally organized jihad.

These selective but influential assessments seem to agree that: global insurgencies have informal structures which are adapted to the characteristics of the Internet; the pattern of linkages between cells is more significant than the cells themselves; a remodelled counter-strategy is needed to address these characteristics rather than a stretched version of national doctrine from the previous century. Kilcullen suggests a big problem facing doctrine writers is the absence of a global authority, which could bring together the states and also the actors from other disciplines that would have to be a part of a counter-strategy. In three individually researched and argued texts, the authors' conclusions are mutually supportive. However, some of these prescriptions are from the perspective of a single discipline and without sufficient peripheral vision of an environment that is perforce intensely international. With a constantly improving picture of the adversary, the next step is a marriage of this analysis with a more realistic assessment of the environment and the friendly actors involved.

The Cohesion Factor

In 2005, globally organized insurgents and local forces working with them demonstrated their continuing potency in the strategic and operational spaces with dramatic acts of violence. Their attacks have developed a virtual energy of their own, swiftly and effortlessly reaching the attention of an international audience of millions. The less visible Internet has also been used with subversive energy by jihadist ideologues connected to the insurgency. However, in the London bombers example, it is not possible to find a structure or model which convincingly links subversion via the Internet in Leeds to a car-bomb offensive in Iraq, to a disembodied voice aired on Al-Jazeera – yet these events have an undeniable strategic coherence.

The previous section identified several writers at the frontlines of research who reached more or less uniform conclusions about the unstructured nature of the Internet, with its multiple forms of communications that link individual nodes to each other, and the correspondingly unstructured organization of the adversary. They all agree that the multiple links between each insurgent individual or cell conform to the multiple links of the Internet. But this description has contradictions. The absence of hierarchy, a leader, an organizational structure and a single manifesto is at odds with the day-to-day evidence of a strategy, a planning capability and a developed system for recruiting, funding, arming and preparing the perpetrators in each attack. In the case of the London bombers, there appeared to be higher tactical intelligence at work, linking one incident to another to create a series of blows against a particular transport system and a particular sector of the commuting population. In the virtual dimension the incidents seemed to be exploiting a deeper animosity aroused by foreign policy abroad and a sense of exclusion at home. Faced by this diversity of incidents, which all seem to point towards a coherent campaign, the temptation is to create what Bruce Hoffman describes as 'a hard wired organogram',[17] a comfortable version of a target, which can be destroyed by using an existing experience and technology. But the greater likelihood is that the relationship between these incidents is casual, their strategic coherence is not planned and we are facing an adversary that grows organically and acts intuitively. It is more like a virus and to defeat it we will have to reorganize our security structures and prepare for an unfamiliar modus operandi. There is also a daunting possibility that the toughest problems in this campaign will be in a virtual territory where the opposition is already well established.

Cohesion Illusion

In its 5 August 2005 edition, *The New York Times* published three stories, 'Britain Goes on High Alert',[18] Al-Jazeera broadcast Zawahiri threats of more attacks[19] and from Baghdad, car bombings on the banks of the River Euphrates.[20] Published together in the same newspaper, these stories have a strategic coherence that suggests oversight by a single commander. However, this assumption is not confirmed by an analysis of the concurrent media or official statements.[21] Even in the London incidents, the two different groups involved have not yet been formally connected to each other. The 7 July bombers were Pakistani-British, with the exception of Germain Lindsay.[22] Directly prior to their attack, they lived in the suburbs of Leeds in Yorkshire. The second group, whose attack failed on 21 July, were from Eritrea and Somalia, with a completely different circle of friends and relatives living in South London, Birmingham and Rome, where they were respectively arrested.[23] Meanwhile, on the banks of the Euphrates, car and suicide bombings, in particular, have tended to be the work of foreign fighters who, in this area, are mainly Saudis and Egyptians entering Iraq from Syria.[24] Finally, the anonymously delivered video of Zawahiri originates from a fourth group of separately organized insurgents.

Exponents of Net war can explain these separate events as the efforts of distinct groups of actors in each location; the mutually reinforcing nature of what happens in the London underground, Iraq and on Al-Jazeera is not the consequence of a single intelligent organization or a deliberate campaign plan. Their apparent coherence is a random convergence of individual groups responding to the same impulse, a mutually experienced rage, admiration of a particular leader, the thrall of an intoxicating idea that explains the world.[25] The problem with this almost plausible explanation of coherence is that the Net war version fails to recognize the significance of 'the intoxicating idea'. Its power seems to be crucial to the insurgents' momentum, so pervasive that it uniformly reaches widely separated communities of different ethnicity and so powerful that it takes men from their wives, families and otherwise normal lives to commit appalling acts against complete strangers.

A recent analysis of the jihadist manifesto 'Knights under the Prophet's Banner' provides a different insight. It explains how Ayman Zawahiri represents a global strategy, a counter-version to Huntington's 'Clash of Civilizations'. In it, Zawahiri proclaims that a jihadist coalition is taking shape to revenge the leaders of global unbelief, the United States, Russia and Israel; later, it refers to 'a new phenomenon that is gaining ground, young combatants who abandon their families, countries, jobs, property and studies to seek a place in which to carry out jihad for the love of Allah'.[26] This intoxicating idea has been distilled to a simple message: to strike America, the apostate dictators of Muslim countries and all the instruments used to combat Islam. In the minds of Muslim sympathizers it successfully connects the Intifada to the insurgencies in Iraq and Afghanistan. For a completely different audience it also feeds the paranoia of the Western contributor populations in the strategic space; every incident becomes a jihadist attack regardless of its provenance, a hoax parcel bomb containing inert powder automatically achieves strategic coherence as part of the effort 'to strike America'.

Although the prevailing evidence on 5 August points to the acts on the Euphrates River, London and Al-Jazeera as three distinct initiatives, the fact that they are inspired by the same impulse – or, in the minds of news readers around the world, could have been – fastens them together. The bombs in London and in Iraq are easily exploited by a third group of like-minded actors who post their video to an obliging Al-Jazeera. Published together in the same newspaper on the same day, they convey a sense of deliberate planning and an ability to act simultaneously at every level. In the case of the Madrid bombings in 2004,[27] the naturally converging results of the act were sufficient to overturn Spanish foreign policy commitments at the strategic level and in the operational space caused the withdrawal of their contingent in Iraq. In his wildest dreams, Mao could not have imagined an insurgent campaign with such globally effective results. In his long-term, labour-intensive strategies, the scale of preparation to achieve a series of blows on this scale against a global 'War on Terror' would have been enormous. Today the synergy of the Internet and the thrall of an intoxicating idea have replaced vertical structures and elaborate campaign plans; impulse is the new strategy, the Internet the new structure.

Faith and the Virtual State
The inventors of the Internet were soon able to point out its relevance to modern insurgency; however, they have been less quick to understand its relationship to absolute forms of religious faith. Hugo Slim[28] and Oliver McTernan condemn the failure to understand the importance of faith, particularly in rich societies driven by the temporal demands of status, income and the need to reproduce. Secular organizations tend to ignore or play down a belief that rejects the free-market virtues of industry, wealth and good living inherent in their own culture. Fascism and communism are repugnant although comprehensible, but infidels, holy lands and heavenly virgins are not the stuff of serious analysis.[29]

Rather than attempt to enter the mind of the subverted bomber, it is easier to rationalize the act as a form of exploitation. It is easier to accept the political aims of jihad than the power of the faith that feeds it, because for the secular analysts, the effort of understanding almost becomes a denial of their own secular lifestyle. From the perspective of the Islamist activist, Slim argues that a faith of such intensity as to cause the rejection of secular values, involves a submission to God's will, the unshakeable knowledge that He will prevail. Everyday life is overwhelmed by the parallel reality of a divine purpose for the world. Following God with such intensity becomes a paradox: individuals have everything when they have nothing, are strongest when they are weakest.[30] Slim, however, warns that there is a connection between living in a state of parallel reality and having a detached view of death. Martyrdom is not always a loud violent protest; it is also the calm abdication of life evinced by the photo[31] of four young men with their explosive packages hanging casually from their shoulders as they entered Luton station at 0721 on Thursday 7 July. Mohammad Sidiquie, the special-needs teacher from Dewsbury, could only have existed in some parallel world that allowed him to contemplate his terrible self-destruction at Edgware Road while he sat among his young pupils in the other reality of the school room in West Yorkshire.

Living in a parallel world of the mind is a solitary affair that is reciprocal to the lifestyle of a habitual Internet user. The solitude and vulnerability of a young man facing the paradox of God and the materialist society around him is eased, but at the same time exploited, by the disembodied personalities and ideas he encounters on the Internet. Bin Laden and the jihadist 'cyber-sheikhs'[32] who support and amplify his message have created a mass of virtual followers, who to some extent live in parallel worlds. They can escape from the day-to-day problems of job, rent, social exclusion into the virtual community of a website and be galvanized by the personality and teachings of a salafist preacher.[33] In a Muslim country, the sheikh engaging with the earnest questions of a believer is a traditional relationship. By transferring this discussion to a website, the devout Muslim in Leeds can continue a relationship with a disembodied religious leader in the virtual dimension. Each website becomes a community in which its leader will address personal and troubling issues with followers on an individual basis.[34]

Becoming disengaged from the temporal demands of living in a real state is also to become part of an alternative state. A crude prototype in revolutionary terms is the Maoist construct of the state within a state. As rebel forces seize more and more populated territory, they impose their own revolutionary forms of governance, taxes and order. Versions of Mao's prototype state within a state continue to this day with spectacular visibility[35] in Nepal and Colombia. In both cases, the rebel held no-go areas or states are defined by territory and, to some extent, the homogeneity of their populations.

However, in a jihadist insurgency, the alternative state takes several forms. In Kilcullen's example,[36] territorial integrity has never been a condition for the displaced refugee and migrant Muslim populations; nevertheless, his Islamist 'virtual state' occupies an area of *terra firma* that lies beyond the writ of government in tribal areas and in the black holes that exist in failed states and abandoned territories. The communities are parasitical, living off resources and vestiges of an infrastructure that were once owned and maintained by the host government. In this form of a state within a state, the centre of gravity is a subverted or disaffected population. Government forces may overrun the areas in which they live but, when the troops leave, the hard-core fighters re-emerge and the alternative structures reassert themselves. Kilcullen's definition is to some extent misnamed for the community, and the territories on which they exist are more real than virtual. Muslims within a strong, functioning host state that does not tolerate no-go areas inside its territory, as in the case in most EU countries, cannot, even if they want to, create a state within a state in the physical sense described above. In UK, the aspiring jihadist therefore becomes part of a genuinely virtual community that largely exists in cyberspace and in the parallel world described earlier.

Olivier Roy insists on a 'deterritorialized version' of Islam, arguing that there is a contradiction between the conventional view of what a Muslim state should be and the real life world 'of migrations, Muslim settlement in non-Muslim countries and the decoupling of religion from given culture and lands'. He maintains that this has culminated in a general 'deterritorialization of Islam'. Nevertheless, among the US-led coalition countries, the fight against Islam is still understood in terms of territory and states, as embodied in the expression 'war on terror'. Roy argues that 'the strategy of the war against terror misses the deterritorialisation element. The concept of a world Muslim Ummah as a geo-strategic actor is nonsense.'[37]

In this description of complex insurgency there are, therefore, several forms of states within states. In the operational space of a jihadist insurgency, within the uncontrolled areas of the host country and the adjoining territories, there are likely to be communities of displaced or excluded elements of a particular population. These populations are real and they occupy actual territory, albeit territory which from time to time may be overrun by government forces. In the strategic space, however, particularly in strong states where the writ of government runs to every corner of its borders, an aspiring jihadist occupies a more virtual state. It largely exists in his or her mind and on the Internet, where virtual leaders and cyber-sheikhs can communicate in a confidential manner to their followers. Individuals living in this virtual state may be subverted and become activists with the same facility as individuals living in the real circumstances of an abandoned territory in the operational area; only the methodology and the hardware for their subversion are different.

Temporal Linkages
Net war exponents describe the Internet as a communication tool and as a place for strangers with common interests to meet and develop a relationship. The power of faith and the community of a virtual state explain how vulnerable or angry individuals can be persuaded by complete strangers and the intoxication of an idea to leave their real life family, job and community and destroy themselves. However, the bombers described above are extreme cases; there is a larger community of supporters who overtly

and lawfully participate each day in the real world around them, but at the same time clandestinely assist insurgent groups through the Internet and in real terms during the preparation of an attack. In many cases, these supporters agree to help strangers from another country or culture in what may turn out to be a fatally dangerous association. What compels individual supporters to enter into a relationship with a complete stranger that they know will lead to the risk of death? Trust and cohesion between individuals, cells and nodes seems to be essential to the momentum of a complex insurgency. Its global, cross-cultural character seems to be unique to Islamist activism and hard to relate to the temporal bonds that underwrite commercial transactions and the multitude of deals that take place in a secular society each day. Absolute faith and a shared religion are huge factors, but there are important temporal linkages which help to foster an initial trust which needs to be considered in addition to the bare wire diagrams of Internet connections.

For jihadists who are divided by language and ethnicity, a shared view of history is important; it might imply a mutual narrative of the partition of Israel, the Palestinian uprisings, the 'War on Terror', the apostate dictators of the Muslim countries and the ultimate establishment of a Caliphate. The manifestos of Qutb, Mawdudi and Abdullah Azam also act as reinforcing and inspiring mutual ideologies. The text of the Qur'an and its study in Arabic compel a degree of cultural uniformity between Muslims of different languages and ethnicities. In addition to a mutual ideology, many clandestine supporters are connected to each other through family and friends spread across the world, living in cities wherever their cultural diaspora is established. According to Kilcullen, intermarriage between Muslim communities of different countries cements the jihadist alliances between theatres.[38] The international structures and linkages of small family businesses, which are lawfully established in different countries, also reinforce relationships between individuals living in separated theatres of Islamist insurgency.

A byproduct of Al-Qa'ida's organizing function is to strengthen linkages between groups and individuals. Al-Qa'ida is not a structured or military organization. It has no vertical linkages attaching frontline activists to distant organizers and commanders. Osama bin Laden has no fighting strength that can be measured in numbers of rebel fighters; he may issue fatwas but he does not marshal together forces to attack, and more important, his eradication will not extinguish the continuing threat of Islamist jihad. As described above, the impetus for Islamic activism is bottom-up. Jason Burke[39] sees Bin Laden as a facilitator, providing an ideology, which translates local passion into acts of terrorism. The shadowy catalyst groups act as commissioning agents, making funds and expertise available to individual cells that have identified a vulnerable target in their own area and have the energy to exploit the situation. In each theatre of Islamist insurgency there are similar facilitating groups whose visits and liaison activities add to the coherence of extreme forms of Islamic activism. Their agents, like the agents of a franchise, travel across borders to bring intelligence, cash and vital expertise, particularly concerning the use of explosives, to enthusiastic activists at the grass-root level. During its debut, in the consciousness of Western observers, Al-Qa'ida was seen as a vertically structured organization that masterminded each attack. However, this perception has been overtaken by the bottom-up model described above, in which the energy for a particular attack arises from disaffected individuals in each community. Al-Qa'ida and similar organizations disseminate their technical experience as well as promoting further introductions and deadly associations.

*

Defining Complex Insurgency

In July 2001, two months before the attacks on New York and Washington, the UK Ministry of Defence published this definition of insurgency in its Army Field Manual series:

> [The] actions of a minority group within a state who are intent on forcing political change by means of a mixture of subversion, propaganda and military pressure, aiming to persuade or intimidate the broad mass of people to accept such a change.[40]

It was qualified by several statements that recognized conditions were changing.

> Until recently it would be true to say that only an insurgency which was capable of attracting widespread popular support posed a real threat to a state's authority. Arms proliferation, and in particular the availability of weapons of mass destruction, together with the possibility of exaggeration through the media of an insurgent's aspirations and prospects could necessitate a reassessment of the threat posed by insurgent groups in the future. While the overall authority of the state may not be at risk, a state's ability to handle the potential disruption imposed by these new issues could have a destabilising effect on any government.

At that time and in that context, this definition and its qualifications were authoritative. They represented a long-term process of distillation of suggestions from military and academic staff and, despite the political oversight of a government ministry, this gave them greater authority than the definitions provided by individuals and even analysts from terrorism research centres.

Two months later the political context changed; the Western world was compelled to recognize the reality of globally organized insurgents and Coalition forces moved across the threshold from containment to intervention. The events which so closely followed the publication of the July 2001 British Army's field manual on counter insurgency operations were destined to change many of our long-held convictions about the nature of insurgency. The UK Army's July definition had become obsolete. At ground level, many of the tactical principles which governed the actions of military forces at the cutting edge of an insurgency remained the same, but above the day-to-day actions in the field, the strategic context had changed. Coalition states were forced to recognize that insurgency had an international dimension which exposed them to terrible acts of terrorism. Nevertheless, the development of a genuinely international counter-strategy was long in gestation. After several years, Coalition nations still do not agree that the hostile forces, which are so visible in the operational space, are part of a much wider network that stretches across the strategic space, that the counter-strategy has to consider the operational, the strategic and the virtual dimension as one concept, and above all, that the campaign also involves a host of international actors in addition to the military force.

A revised, internationally acceptable doctrine also has to recognize the importance of ideology. Communism, national self-determination and the political movements of the last century inspired a degree of passion but not to an extreme that launches multiple suicide attacks. Complex insurgency is also characterized by the absolute and intense nature of the faith of its followers, as distinguished from the secular determination of national insurgents in the Cold War period. Jonathon Stevenson[41] characterized this difference as 'old terrorism' and 'new terrorism'. 'Old terrorists' are motivated by temporal aspirations: freedom, statehood, cultural separatism and a long-term prospect of negotiations and a credible end state. 'New terrorists' act in a more impulsive manner. Their end state does not lend itself to being translated to a series of negotiable objectives. It is absolute and reads more like a cry for havoc or perhaps, as some analysts point out, a cry for help from a deeply distressed society.

An effective doctrine has to recognize that the critical battle is, in this case, for the Muslim mind, and that the source of power, which energizes the insurgency, springs from the subverted or converted element of a distressed population. It has to recognize intense faith as the cohesion factor of the insurgency, reinforcing bonds between strangers, giving impetus to the spread of information and adding an appearance of cohesion to what might otherwise be random acts of violence. The engine rooms of this insurgent power lie among the oppressed, displaced and outraged communities; the battle is for the mind of the would-be activist.

This final section of Chapter Two summarizes the characteristics of a global or complex insurgency with a view to creating a definition. It also sets out to relate these findings to the conclusions reached in Chapter One concerning the different spaces of the campaign (strategic, operational and virtual) and the nature of the vital ground in each space. The obstacle in the path of creating a generic model is that there is at present only one example of global insurgency – namely, the current jihadist campaign. The definition at the conclusion of this section is nevertheless written in a generic form.

Complex insurgency in the strategic space

As defined earlier the strategic space refers to the world that lies beyond the operational area where the international coalition is engaged in a counter insurgency campaign. The strategic space is significant because it contains the HQs of international organizations, the states contributing to the coalition forces and the Muslim states, which all have a part to play in the campaign. Insurgents have successfully targeted the relationship between a national contingent in the operational space, its mainstream population at home, its national media and its current government, which will in due course have to submit itself for re-election. In this matrix the population is the vital ground for both the insurgent and the leaders of the government. The insurgent tactic is to locate and facilitate the disaffected parts of a migrant community and encourage it to attack its host population. Their purpose is to demoralize the contributor state's mainstream population. The attacks, which are designed to kill large numbers of civilians, have an inherent quality of horror and drama, which energizes the dissemination of related images across the world. They dishearten the coalition states and embolden the insurgents and elements of their supporting populations. In the recent attack on London, however, the immediate effect was to strengthen British political resolve not to withdraw. Nevertheless a spontaneous consequence of the attack has been the sudden rise in intercommunal tension in the UK, which may later act as the recruiting sergeant for the insurgency. The insurgents' relationship to the minority element of the same contributing state, which may be hovering on the brink of supporting their cause, obviously has to be different. It is a relationship that has many different facets ranging from pastoral exchanges between religious leaders and their followers to the operational mechanics of organizing a bomb attack.

As described earlier, the connections and linkages in this multifaceted exchange are unstructured and arise from the nature of the Internet and its characteristic as a meeting place. Despite the jihadist facilitators' apparent warmth towards the volunteers, they regard them as highly expendable. The shadowy figures, who arrive with funds and expertise to arrange the attack, will leave directly for another operation, but the local actors will either die in their efforts or be 'hung out to dry' for the police. Regardless of this outcome, the energy for further attacks continues to arise from the grass roots of the migrant population. The spontaneous, disparate, unstructured characteristic of these efforts is moderated by the unifying impositions of their faith. In addition a common historical and religious ideology gives random insurgent attacks a strategic coherence. This helps to relate an attack on a strategic population to the campaign in the operational space; the connection may be casual but its impact is convincingly manoeuvrist and has the effect of forcing the coalition into a reactive posture.

Complex insurgency at the operational level
The operational space refers to the area where coalition forces have intervened to restore the territory of a state to a legitimate government in order to prevent its further use as a sanctuary for global insurgents. The epicentre is the host state, Afghanistan or Iraq, and at the edges of the operational space will be populations connected to the conflict, as well as the logistic entry points used by the international response. The insurgents' purpose in the operational space is to deny the coalition forces, and the associated civil agencies, the secure use of the territory and prevent the restoration of a legitimate form of government. The insurgent campaign in the operational space has a similarly impulsive character to that in the strategic space. There are three forms of insurgent activity – local, national and international – referring to the activities of foreign fighters.

The locally recruited insurgents are closer to road bandits than genuine revolutionaries. In many cases they were already involved in crime before being enlisted for an insurgent purpose. In Iraq, substantial elements were previously common criminals released from jail in the chaotic circumstances of the 2003 intervention. In both Afghanistan and Iraq, opportunistic association with clans engaged in cross-border trafficking may provide manpower and local knowledge for a particular attack. The local insurgent is characteristically untrained and learns about weaponry and clandestine living on the job. His interests are venal and short term. After each attack he hopes to be richer; personal gain is his primary motivation, and therefore his information and services need to be bought. He is more driven by cash than faith. Besides his contracts with the jihadist elements of the insurgency, he is likely to have a continuing interest in the traffic of narcotics, weapons, money and even humans. In the operational space, the income arising from criminal activities, particularly narcotics, which could be locally grown and distributed on an industrial scale, is used to fund the insurgency. There is, therefore, a growing relationship between organized crime and the insurgency. Locally, there appears to be no moral contradiction between the source of the funds and their ultimate purpose. The relationship of a criminal, engaged for the time being on an insurgent mission, towards the host population is predatory.

The national insurgents in Iraq have several derivations, which are largely connected with their previous functions in, and loyalty to, the former regime, and in Afghanistan they may be similarly associated with the Taliban. In both cases their aim is to prevent the coalition from succeeding in its effort to re-monopolize violence into the hands of an elected government. National insurgents may be former intelligence officers, police, security forces and, more recently, recruited fighters. They are therefore distinct form the lumpen road bandit. Their targets include the government, coalition forces and the humanitarian programmes seeking to create a more secure civil society. For a national insurgent, a successful foreign intervention, a popular government and a civil society spell the end of his previous power and lead to retribution. A more democratic and secular population also threatens the traditional clan structures and the enforcement of Sharia law. In Zawahiri's strategic concept for jihad, the UN humanitarian actors and international non-governmental organizations funded by the populations concerned with the coalition are seen as the instruments to combat Islam.[42] At operational level this edict has significance to the national insurgents. If the humanitarian programmes succeed, the national insurgency is terminally threatened. Although the high-value target is the coalition military force, it is also a most protected and dangerous target to engage. Therefore, the insurgent will lower his priorities to include NGOs, civil agencies, media and individuals from the contributing states. The national insurgent is less flagrantly venal than the road bandit; he has a longer-term purpose and does not expect a personal gain after each attack. His relationship to the population is ambiguous. He needs their support, he relies on their reluctance to co-operate with the coalition, he uses them as a refuge, but in the former regime he was accustomed to an abusive relationship in which he was the habitual abuser.

The international jihadist is a manifest linkage between the operational and the strategic. He arrives in the operational space, having been found, recruited, trained and moved into the theatre by a convergence of clandestine cells and individuals which lies beyond the operational space. He is by background and ethnicity distinct from the local and national insurgent. His motives for volunteering are largely inspired by faith and passion. His ambitions are strategic: to strike America, the apostate rulers and the coalition forces in accordance with Zawahiri's concept for jihad. His attitude and methods may be different, but in the operational area he will be launched against the same target list as the national insurgent. He is unlikely to have a developed relationship with the local population and has to be more able to sustain himself. Western analysts see an important schism between the foreign fighters and the indigenous insurgents. At present this does not seem to unduly degrade their capacity for offensive operations significantly.

During the 1990s, the military opposition to the containment forces that deployed to the collapsed states of Eastern Europe, Sub-Saharan Africa and Asia took several forms in terms of its motivation and capability. The distinction of the 1990s containment scenario is that the opposition in a particular host state was monolithic and all its manifestations would conform to a particular type of insurgency. For example, in Southern Sudan, Sierra Leone or Liberia the opposition forces were organized like, and their modus operandi was closer to, the local insurgents described above, whereas in Sri Lanka, Colombia and Nepal they have the capabilities and long-term aspirations and organization of a popular or national insurgency. The characteristic of complex insurgency is that *different* categories of insurgency are now manifested together in the *same* operational space even in the same town, for example in Falluja. The potentially divisive motivations and different degrees of religious passion are submerged beneath their overwhelming mutual concern to resist the foreign invader.

The RAND study describes the process, which integrates the armed elements of different insurgent and survival philosophies into a single group for a particular operation, as the Federated Insurgency Complex (FIC).[43] Integration merges the experience and resources of various individuals and groups into a single complex. It may comprise functional groups which individually smuggle weapons, launder money and have a developed training capability. It may be a convergence of resources and intelligence. The sum of these assets is an operational force, constituted from very different individuals who are tenuously linked together for the period of a particular attack. There is no hard wiring or leadership structure. The glue which holds them together may be the jihad, a common narrative of recent history, a fierce animosity for the foreign occupation or the prospect of reward.

The Virtual Dimension
This definition concerns only the populations of the contributing states, the host state and the Muslim minorities who constitute the vital ground. The conflict in the virtual dimension refers to the struggle to alter the minds of specific populations in a way that supports either the strategic aims of the insurgents or the initiatives of the leaders that oppose them. The virtual dimension also refers to the communications systems and media that can be used to reach the minds of these populations, together with the ideas, images and key communicators that can alter their beliefs.

If we were faced by a deliberative, vertically organized insurgent structure, its objectives in the virtual dimension would be to: demoralize the populations of the contributing state; embolden the Muslim minorities within them; subvert the vulnerable; and galvanize the uncommitted to take action. Real life jihadists do not have such formal structures or deliberative approaches, but the natural energy of their movement and the proliferation of communication systems deliver many of these objectives for them in any case. It is the obliging Western media that created the icons of this insurgency, not the jihadist fighters. Constant repetition has turned the images of the Twin Towers, Guantanamo Bay, Abu Ghraib and Camp Bread Basket into the symbols of their cause. Their subliminal impact no longer requires a text or even a caption. The best photos of Osama bin Laden, depicted sympathetically as the desert pimpernel, dressed in terrorist chic, cradling the *de rigueur* AK-47, have reached the widest possible audiences through Western media.

The offensive action in the virtual dimension by jihadist elements is of a considerably lesser scale. Using the Internet, jihadist agencies have succeeded in subverting, galvanizing and organizing individuals in the same key Muslim minorities, and these have acted with devastating effect in isolated cases. Key communicators in hiding, kidnappers and clandestine organizations successfully exploit the events in the strategic and operations space. These efforts are not always effective. The baroque statements of a distant Bin Laden aide or an Al-Qa'ida surrogate fail to communicate to audiences that are influenced by the symbols and phraseology of their own culture. Bin Laden's greatest hits are delivered for him to the strategic populations by the Western media, using the familiar language and news anchor personalities that they have grown to accept as authoritative. Both the insurgent jihadists and the coalition states which oppose them can exploit the strong relationship between the operational, the strategic and the vertical; but the insurgents have done it more successfully. Most of their success in the virtual dimension is due to the nature of the dimension itself and the proliferating, amplifying effect it has on a dramatic incident. However, jihadist agencies have also established themselves in the Internet ahead of the forces which oppose them. From this position they exploit the characteristics of the Internet in a manoeuvrist fashion that relates the strategic to the operational which is boosted and promulgated by a media that claims to represent all creeds and political colours.

*

New versions of insurgency were already emerging prior to 9/11, but since that event, the visibility of the insurgent, and the massive response by coalition forces, has compelled a more intensive reappraisal of our existing beliefs and principles. This definition sets out to distinguish *complex insurgency* from the nationally-oriented forms of insurgency that arose in the previous century. It also sets out to show that a complex insurgency has important differences in its structure and use of space, which in turn impose a different counter-strategy.

- A complex insurgency is a campaign by globally dispersed activists and insurgents who seek to confront the culture and political ideals of a nation or group of nations that are seen to challenge their interests and way of life.
- The insurgent is assisted by the nature and energy of the virtual dimension and exploits it by growing in a networked configuration and executing kinetic attacks whose images reach an audience of

millions of concerned individuals.
- It is more important for globally organized insurgent forces to alter the beliefs and policies of the opposed populations than to seize territory or to overthrow a particular government with the purpose of replacing it with one representing the global movement.
- The conflict may take the form of subversion that leads to acts of terrorism. The insurgents seek to demoralize the civilian populations of the states that oppose them by threats and terrorism against their presence anywhere in the world.

3. A Disunited International Response

Chapter Two explains how the characteristics of the complex insurgent compel us to rethink our counter-strategy. It describes the activists as a tiny minority impelled by the same inspiring faith or manifesto. Despite the absence of co-ordinating or leadership structures, the universality of their faith and their intent gives their disparate attacks the semblance of coherence. This linkage causes governments of contributor states to react defensively, conferring a manoeuvrist effect on the insurgent act, but in reality the action-reaction linkage is seldom the result of a deliberate plan. The configuration of a complex insurgency, however, offers little prospect of a manoeuvrist counter-strategy, particularly in current military thinking and the preoccupation for effects-based warfare. The insurgents work in leaderless, unstructured networks, which form and reform into federated groups according to need; these do not present themselves as targets in a conventional or kinetic sense.

In the popular interpretation of the 'war on terror', the frontlines of the conflict are represented as the violent areas of Iraq and Afghanistan. This perception seems to survive, despite the acts of terrorism in the strategic areas against the concerned populations, which might emphasize that there are no front lines. A more realistic assessment is that the strategic is linked to the operational via the virtual, and news and images from the London and New York media may translate into rioting and bomb blasts in the streets of Baghdad and Kandahar. Similarly, violence against individuals and non-combatant organizations in the field influence their distant directorates in New York[1] and Geneva. The drama and the horror of insurgent atrocities against the civil population, and the coalition's military operations, provide a narrative and an imagery that become the icons and the mythology of the conflict. So far the processes and products of the virtual dimension seem to favour the insurgent, not the coalition effort.

Chapter Three returns to the original proposition, which is that despite the enthusiasm of coalition military forces for manoeuvre, it is in fact the insurgent forces who have succeeded in taking the initiative. The reasons for this are complicated. The functional sectors of the international response correspond to the non-military tasks in the operational area. An array of civil agencies, military forces, police and national institutions are involved; they represent the tools to rebuild a nation from its political leaders at the top, right down to the local school and the village policeman in the remote areas. Although the response, whose task it is to rebuild these facilities, is sometimes portrayed as a community, it is in reality more a convergence of independently motivated and organized actors. Because of their disparate nature, the sum of these efforts is unwieldy, the response lacks moral coherence, is not able to act decisively and therefore cannot take a manoeuvrist approach, assuming there was an opportunity to do so. Nevertheless, the civil agencies in the response play an essential part in the effort to win popular support. In the description that follows, the characteristics of the operational space are largely generic and derived from aspects of Afghanistan and Iraq.

Actors in the Operational Space

After the initial intervention to seize the host country is over, the warfighting elements of the coalition become the occupying power[2] in a state that in most respects is dysfunctional. Its former government has fled, its police and military forces are in disarray and its infrastructure has been destroyed, first of all by the intervention, and subsequently looted down to its foundations by vengeful locals. Schools, hospitals, water, power, communications and the economy have ceased to function, leaving the population on the edge of survival.

It is, therefore, in the context of a much wider crisis in the operational space that the insurgent groups described above have emerged. Consequently, the response or the counter-strategy cannot be a narrow military affair, which merely seeks the attrition of the adversary. The vital ground or the host population is in immediate need of a wide range of requirements in addition to their security from armed attack. It is a list, which will take at least a decade to deliver and is beyond the resources of a single actor, no matter how rich or powerful. The aim of the intervention may be to restore a monopoly of violence into the hands of a legitimate host government. But within that overarching purpose there are more precise objectives concerning the restoration of the vital organs of the state, civil society and the economy. These also include the development of political parties and the organization of an election. The international response represents the physical diversity of these tasks, as well as the diversity of experience needed to survey and design an effective restoration process. There are therefore several broad sectors of capability.

- *Military:* The configuration of foreign military contingents in the operational space will alter with the different phases of the campaign. After the initial invasion, the combat forces led by the US reorganize into an occupying garrison. The host state will be subdivided into military areas, which have a degree of autonomy, particularly if they are occupied by a single nation within the coalition, as in the case of the British in Basra. In addition to the coalition forces, there may be an international force, which is authorized under a different mandate and controlled by a different international HQ. In a future scenario it is possible that a UN force may be located in the same area as a US-led coalition.

- *Bilateral donors:* Concerned states or contributor states provide the contingents, which make up the military coalition with the US. In many cases they also comprise the bulk of the bilateral donors which provide the funds and the oversight for the development and nation-building programmes. In either case they will establish embassies in the capital of the host state. In addition to their normal diplomatic function, these embassies exercise a supervisory presence over their own bilateral programmes, as well as providing oversight for the element of their own forces that is in a quasi-military role. They also have an important information-gathering role. In the cases of the largest donors, individual government departments may exercise a stove-pipe relationship with their assets in the operational space which sometimes diminishes the coherence of what is intended to be a joint counter-strategy. An international organization such as the EU or the OSCE may also be a bilateral donor, and will establish a similar presence as a concerned nation. Each bilateral donor is therefore autonomous to some degree and can exercise its individual influence on the overall strategy.

- *The UN system:* Strictly speaking, the UN is regarded as an international organization; however, it is explained here as a separate system that has many different manifestations in the operational space, each of which is usually autonomous, separately funded and separately directed from a HQ in Rome, Geneva or New York. The UN Security Council may be represented by a Special Representative of the Secretary General (SRSG) who will be autonomous within the host country and have his or her own HQ and staff.[3] The SRSG may exercise a degree of oversight on the activities of at least five or six major UN Agencies concerned with food, health, children, refugees, human rights and development. These agencies will run humanitarian and development programmes in their own functional sectors. There may also be UN administration units to oversee the elections and assist with the regeneration of a government.

- *International organizations:* There are a number of major, globally established organizations whose idiosyncratic status and function in the operational space require them to be considered in a separate category. These include: the International Red Cross and Red Crescent; the International Organization for Migration; the World Bank; the International Monetary Fund; and the World Trade Organization. Each is separately funded and has its own charter and independent directorate. Each brings important assets to the recovery plan, including funding, burden sharing and transparency.
- *Non-governmental organizations:* Depending on the security in areas beyond the envelope held by the coalition, there could be more than a hundred NGOs in the operational space. In the context of a proxy war zone, NGOs face problems of funding and freedom of movement. Their different response to these problems is beginning to divide them into two categories, multi-mandated NGOs and strictly humanitarian NGOs. Medecins Sans Frontier (MSF) is a notable example in the latter category. MSF strive to maintain an independent position in the operational space that allows them to access all communities and actors irrespective of whether they are pro-insurgency, pro-coalition or pro-host nation. The strictly humanitarian lobby have an important function in a proxy war zone where the actors and population are frequently compelled to take sides in the conflict. Their strenuous efforts to remain uncommitted in this respect allow them to rescue and communicate with communities and individuals who are otherwise beyond the reach of the international response. Because the strictly humanitarian agencies see themselves as increasingly linked to a response which is politically committed to a counter-strategy, some have begun (MSF in the Democratic Republic of Congo) to distinguish themselves by using pink-coloured vehicles, as opposed to white ones. MSF have reinforced their independent status by funding themselves as far as

possible from impartial public donations of which less than 20 per cent of the total is from government sources. Multi-mandated NGOs tend to work closer to the contributor states that fund the rebuilding programmes. Nevertheless, they are also wary of finding themselves irretrievably linked to the coalition side and are organizing their own security which enables them to move independently of the military, as they do in Afghanistan, for example.[4]

- *Private security companies and contractors:* A characteristic of a proxy war zone is the increasing presence of private companies, which provide their services to national contributors, their military forces as well as to the civil agencies. Private security companies protect convoys, co-ordinate movements and provide close protection for personnel and resources, as opposed to the 'service providers' that supply power, food, water, fuel, shelter and repairs to the military intervention forces. Private companies are increasingly moving into NGO areas of competence, where they have taken on the reconstruction of schools, hospitals, providing water as well as the distribution of vaccines and food.[5] This particular dimension of their employment, however, is linked to the military campaign to win over the population. Private companies are also increasing their involvement in the Security Sector Reform programmes by training police, military and government officials for the host state. Although humanitarian and development officials vociferously resist the private sector encroachment into their territory, it would seem to be an inevitable consequence of intervening in a proxy war zone where the expectation of having a secure humanitarian space is at odds with the declared intent of the insurgent forces to attack the humanitarian actors. Furthermore, in the context of a counter-insurgency campaign, the contractual relationship with a private company is more comfortable for a military intervention force.

- *The host government:* As the rebuilding programmes and SSR begin to take effect, the host government should begin to assert itself as the ultimate inheritor of the sectors under reconstruction. These assets include the reorganized national armed forces, police and government administration. The capability and effectiveness of the host government is a crucial factor in counter-insurgency. But it is hard to mobilize popular support behind a rebuilding programme and a military effort to destroy the insurgents if the host government behaves in a way that is palpably unacceptable to the population or ineffec-

- tive in terms of the success of the campaign.
- Finally, *the media* in every form will be present at all levels, creating images and narratives for a global audience. Although seldom received beyond the immediate area of the host state, local media reporting in the languages of the host population play an important part in the campaign. Their target audience is local and their output may be monitored by the host government. In the containment era of the previous decade, international force commanders with a flair for communication used local media to reach the local population.[6] Each contributor state will also have an element of its national media covering the activities of its military contingent and its bilateral programmes. The rest of the world, including the 'Arab street' and the concerned Muslim minorities, is reached via satellite channels.

Degrees of Coherence

In the 1950s, Robert Thompson, a pioneering figure in the development of counter-insurgent strategy, pushed for a holistic response that would give government forces a united front against the 'terrorists'.[7] He argued that to turn the population away from supporting the insurgent required a massive effort by the actors on the government side to become part of a single counter-strategy. This meant that military action was linked to simultaneous measures to improve personal security in the population, local living conditions and a stronger local economy. The physical efforts on the ground carried out by all the different government forces and departments involved were knitted into a single political strategy led by a single civilian appointee. But even in the ideal circumstances of Thompson's national counter-strategy, in Malaya it took more than ten years for his concept to succeed. British doctrine regarded successful counter-insurgency as dependent on compromises between the different elements of the government and the community leaders. The imperatives of a democratic political system, military security, good intelligence, accountability and the personal freedoms of the public seemed to be mutually exclusive. However, compromises were possible because they were amicably struck between the departments and ministries of the same nation, often between longstanding colleagues. The lessons of Malaya have become part of the British institutional wisdom on counter-insurgency and continue to be reflected in current doctrine – in particular, the primacy of political rather than military leadership, the limitations of operating in a democratic society and the need for co-ordination between the elements of the counter-strategy.[8]

But in the post-9/11 strategic era, where a complex insurgency becomes a global problem and the counter-strategy has to involve the disparate elements of an international response described above, there appear to be many reasons why Thompson's approach may not succeed. In the deadly tension that emerges between the complex insurgents, the host government, the civil population and the international response, the complex insurgent seems to have a number of unassailable advantages. His message has a directness and simplicity to 'strike the American Coalition' or, referring particularly to the international NGOs, to 'strike the instruments used against Islam'.[9] Under the rousing effect of these banners, the schisms between the local, national and international elements of the federated insurgent complex are less apparent. The universality of their battle cry gives a semblance of coherence to their individually planned and executed attacks. This, together with an intensely shared faith, provides the metaphorical glue that bonds them long enough to plan and launch an attack. The international element of the FIC understands how to take advantage of strategic space. The complex insurgents therefore have a number of connections and leverages to canvass and exploit the support of all the populations, which are also for them the vital ground.

A host population's priorities are closer to Maslow's hierarchy of human needs than the promises of the insurgent or the versions of democracy imported by the development programmes in all their forms. The members of a household want security and to enjoy the fundamental condition of not living in a war zone where their lives, possessions and sources of income may be terminated at any moment. Security for them is freedom from the depredations of the local gang or a malevolent warlord. Security is also having electricity, water, a local school, access to medical treatment and a job.[10] A dispossessed population is ambivalent about who provides these conditions. They do not care if their survival rations come from the impeccably correct Red Cross or the deeply manipulative US Special Forces. They feel just as secure living in a village owned by a reasonably fair warlord as they would in the areas controlled by the host government and the coalition. It is the quality of life within that envelope of land, which dictates their support and acceptance of the provider.

More by accident than by careful planning, the jihadists have developed a powerful coherence factor. Their variations on the theme of 'strike America' inspire the would-be activist as successfully as it feeds the paranoia of the contributor populations. It is a one-fits-all slogan, a distillation of Zawahiri's manifesto, no doubt redolent with shortcuts and half-truths, but nevertheless a powerfully mobilizing instrument. Against this jihadist sound bite, the extracts referencing the 'war on terror' are miserable failures. Conceived in the passionate aftermath of 9/11, the 'war on terror' manifesto primarily addresses the concerns of a US Republican constituency. However plausible its message may sound to a Texan audience, it translates badly to other cultures and particularly badly to the Muslim minorities in the concerned states and the host populations of Iraq and Afghanistan. According to Gilles Kepel, the US message has missed its target; the neoconservative strategy for the democratization of the 'New Middle East' failed to enlist the support of its highest priority: the Muslim middle classes. Instead, the term 'Western Democracy' has taken on a negative connotation for the very class for whom it held out most benefit.[11] No realistic Coalition general in the operational space imagines that the political aspirations of his counter-strategy could be articulated to a local population on local media using sound bites from the 'war on terror'. There are, instead, host government manifestos and corresponding slogans in Iraq and Afghanistan – but do they convey the same intent as the 'war on terror', or do they, in fact, articulate the tension between the needs of a US-led global strategy and the needs of a Muslim state which has become a proxy war zone.

A successful counter-strategy that reduces the support enjoyed by the insurgent has to recognize the concerned populations as its vital ground.[12] Today, the Coalition's centre of gravity includes Western contributor populations, the Muslim minority communities within them and the host population in the operational space. But the diversity of the Coalition and its associated civil agencies sends mixed signals to the vital ground populations. Even within the Bush administration there have been disabling differences of approach between government departments. Closer to the ground, the sectors of the response have varying rationales for their participation and they do not have a shared view of the 'war on terror'. Most NGOs actively disassociate themselves from President Bush and his administration's 'war on terror' pronouncements. There are no key communicators for the response, no mutual sources of policy or manifestos that are universally respected and no charismatic Bin Laden figure to unite the bickering humanitarians and military forces who continuously find themselves in the same operational spaces. Even within sectors there is disparity, for example between different members of the EU and within individual states. Peace marches, disaffected ambassadors and disgruntled generals are the fabric of democracy, but they reinforce a sense of incoherence. On the opposing side, certain jihadist figures are key communicators – their authority is unimpeachable to the isolated Islamic activist and obliging Arabic satellite channels to promulgate their message to massive Muslim audiences.

The international intervention, in all its forms, has failed to reach the same vital ground with the same compulsion and coherence as its tiny adversary. The melange of contingents and civil agencies in the operational space in some respects resembles its networked enemy. Between the main sectors (military, NGOs, bilateral donors, etc.), and within each sector, there is an absence of hierarchy: the UN's SRSG, the military commanders, the Red Cross delegates and the ambassadors for the bilateral donors have an unstructured, horizontal relationship. Like the insurgents, the international response also forms into federations to carry out a particular programme; however, the glue that holds them together is less powerful. They have no common ideological view of their collective role in the host state, and there are well-known differences of approach between the humanitarian sectors and the military. In 2004 the Inter-Agency Standing Committee (IASC) updated its guidance to humanitarian actors involved with Coalition forces. Their instruction enjoins all humanitarian practitioners to keep away from Coalition military forces, not to share information, not to use military assets or transport, to avoid the use of military escorts whenever possible and to continuously maintain their independence. This emphasizes several unresolved problems in the humanitarian-military relationship. Some military commanders continue to have a natural preference for the dimension of the campaign that is closest to their professional comfort zone and engages their massive technical superiority. This may win for them the kinetic part of the conflict but that does not amount to succeeding in the overall campaign. After the highly successful US action in Falluja, a June 2005 military report described the town as 'an angry disaster', where the police stations were planned but barely started, roads remained unpaved, a train station that was still mined and trains that could not function. Falluja needed bulldozers, workers and cement rather than cash.[13]

Commanders at most levels recognize that the population in the operational space is their vital ground[14] and that winning them over to their side requires more than the provision of military security, such as providing water, power, schools, hospitals and a livelihood. But the problem has been to connect a successful military campaign to a less dynamic civil programme to restore the infrastructure; under day-to-day stress and pressures from above, commanders cease to understand that restoring a quality of life, rather than counting bodies, is the campaign winning factor.

The problem is that the military and some government departments, particularly in Washington, see the humanitarian actors as 'force multipliers' and part of the overall strategy.[15] But the humanitarian practitioners see themselves, especially the ones who relate to the IASC's recent injunction, as part of a completely separate programme. This is more than an absence of glue, these are completely different views of what is happening in the same operational space, and despite the superficial structures in many armies[16] for civil-military co-operation (CIMIC), humanitarians have an unremitting resistance to being co-opted into a counter-strategy.

In Afghanistan and Iraq, the jihadist in the operational space has the advantage of having a direct relationship to the virtual and the strategic. From beyond the operational space he receives manpower, funds, logistics, intelligence and stimulating images that he can exploit. The problem for the military force commander who opposes him is that the Coalition is limited by vertical boundaries imposed by a vertical interpretation of the conflict. The sources of the jihadis's energy are beyond the coalition's horizon; the commander has no practical concept whereby he can merge the operational, the strategic and the virtual to his advantage. In the operational space the military force is in a consistently reactive posture waiting for foreign fighters that will arrive from the strategic space that is beyond their reach.[17] They have no control over the policies that result in negative stories from Guantanamo Bay and Abu Ghraib that arouse violence in their battalion areas.

From the perspective of an analyst it appears that the campaign in the operational space is at an awkward developmental stage between two concepts. The traditional version of our doctrine recognizes the supportive attitude of the population as the tipping factor for both the insurgent and the government forces. In traditional British thinking, a successful counter-insurgent campaign requires compromises and sometimes these require making concessions to the insurgents' political intent.[18] The operational art in previous national campaigns was to requisition the insurgent's most potent political banners and adopt them into a democratic solution that would become the political counter-strategy. But in British experience this required the players in the counter-strategy to work as a team. A future version of counter-insurgent doctrine has to be international and multi-layered in its scope. The coherence and structure of the response have to be altered; a stretched version of the traditionalist approach cannot succeed in Iraq or Afghanistan. On the Coalition side there are too many moving parts in the operational space; they lack cohesion and co-ordination. Their incoherence affects the outcome of the campaign and is exploited by the insurgent.

The humanitarians seem to face a similar crisis of concept. Their philosophy and approach worked well in a containment scenario where there was a more credible humanitarian space, but not in a proxy war zone where they are also in the target frame, regardless of the colour of their vehicles. The humanitarian and development tasks are still massively important; the question is whether the traditional humanitarian practitioners as defined and regulated by the IASC are any longer the correct instrument.

Manoeuvre in the Strategic Space

Very few nations can be regarded as completely uninvolved or unconcerned with global jihad. In the strategic space, populations are involved because they are Muslim, or because they are Muslim minorities in a Western contributor state and vulnerable to subversion, or in the case of Western states, because they have contributed military contingents or assets. Olivier Roy adds another dimension to the characterization of vital ground populations by arguing that the core of the jihadist movement is 'de-territorialized', which allows them to move freely and associate as an international body. They prey on Muslims, who are moving towards re-Islamization. According to Roy,[19] the conversion to extreme forms of activism is not achieved by returning to a country of origin or by the local pressures of family, neighbourhood or community. The formerly inert Muslim becomes a participating activist as the result of personal withdrawal and contemplation that is exploited by meeting an influencing personality – the Afghan veteran or the neo-fundamentalist preacher. Roy maintains that the lives of many of these predatory personalities follow a 'de-territorialized trajectory'. The jihadist recruiters and their supporting organizers target second-generation Muslims, exploit their loneliness and sense of victimization. Radical Islamic activism offers a substitute identity as part of a vanguard of international jihad to 'strike America and the instruments against Islam'.

In the context of the current conflict and the recruitment of second-generation immigrants, Kepel sees the Muslim minorities of the EU as standing at a junction. The ideal path would be for the young modern

Muslim to become incorporated into Europe's success, where their growing numbers would be a bastion against Islamic jihad and a stable source of radical criticism against the despotic Muslim regimes in their country of origin. But Kepel's more worrying alternative is for a potentially violent minority to reject cultural integration and embrace separatism, resentment, hatred and extremes of violence.[20] He asks whether radical Islam is a new form of Communism, the entry point for the excluded minority to become part of the national political debate – a substitute for Muslims who see themselves as a European underclass without a secular party or a manifesto under which to unite. Kepel and Roy agree that in the strategic context, the vulnerable minorities, which harbour individual jihadists and offer the environment for their subversion, do not have a territorial identity. They live within a host population and they may be spread around from city to city – their collective personality is virtual: they are an Internet state.

In an intuitive fashion, the insurgent strategy seems to understand this. At the lowest level, along the frontlines of subversion, the jihadist efforts to capture the attention of the vulnerable Muslim immigrant are instinctive and develop organically; they are also very effective. The connection between the excluded individual and the exploitative figures searching for him is casually made, but there is a high chance that it will eventually take place. It may happen at any meeting point: the mosque, the gymnasium, radical bookshop, video exchange, student group, even on a rafting trip. Once the vulnerable recruit meets the influential jihadist figure it will become harder to turn back. The intoxicating idea and the parallel life take over.

The land forces engaged in Iraq and Afghanistan are probably the most powerfully equipped and experienced professional forces that have ever been deployed. But they are part of an alliance, in which there is an absence of moral cohesion and mutual trust that prevents decisive action in the field. There is no concept that allows commanders to move between the strategic, the tactical and the virtual with the same facility as their opponents. The international military instrument reacts well but does not have the tools or the cultural intuition to turn the initiative against the insurgent. The security forces have a solid warlike quality, with vertical structures and hierarchies, but their adversary has none of these and behaves like a virus growing organically and attacking instinctively. Without a head or a heart, it seems to survive every form of amputation.

From the perspective of a conventional military force, the complex insurgents and their global arena have a boundless quality that defies a kinetic counter-strategy. It is possible to define the insurgents and locate their vital ground, but less easy to see how to prevent the one subverting the other. There is a lack of tangibility about the problem.

Somewhere in the strategic space multiple acts of subversion occur every day, on the street or on an Internet screen between the vulnerable victims and the subversive predators. In the scale of the entire campaign they are microscopically tiny occurrences, unseen by next of kin or by the security organizations. They take place far away from the realities of school, work or family, in a bubble of escapism that encloses the victim and the predator. Each successful meeting seems to initiate a process of subversion and activism. Coalition forces and national police divisions appear to have no concept for interrupting the process at this point, for piercing this bubble and releasing the victim from the thrall of the intoxicating idea. The weight of our national force and intelligence effort is poised to react after the subversion has been successful, not to forestall the act itself. In the linear process of disillusion-isolation-subversion-terrorist act, our emphasis is placed on reacting to the last phase, but the manoeuvrist would interrupt the first one.

In such a dynamic form of conflict, are we too conventional in our understanding of manoeuvre and the forces that have the best opportunity to do it? Rather than the armoured squadrons in Falluja, it might turn out to be the Muslim bloggers and the local NGO in Leeds who are better poised to interdict the process of subversion. The insurgent activities in the streets of Birmingham are by perception linked to the car-bomb offensive in Baghdad to achieve a manoeuvrist effect; but constrained by the straitjacket of Cold War thinking, the coalition that opposes him cannot network its assets with the same facility. The local NGOs[21] and the bloggers, who challenge the insurgent process and may be the gateway to a future strategy, are not seen by the coalition powers as part of their inventory.

4. Defeating Complex Insurgency

In its twentieth-century form, counter-insurgency was a gradual Byzantine process that delicately drew together many different government departments into a single strategy. In the post-9/11 era, we find ourselves countering a complex insurgency which has a multi-layered, global characteristic. The circumstances of the present strategic era offer the complex insurgent the opportunity to take a manoeuvrist approach. The counter-strategy becomes as multifaceted and complicated as the opponent it seeks to destroy – in military terms alone it will be a very challenging and long-term operation. But as the task grows more difficult and complicated, the counter-instrument grows less manageable and more disparate in its constitution. The military element becomes internationalized and the civil element mutates into an array of fractious agencies, which do not see themselves as part of a counter-insurgent campaign. This coalition of disparate actors is too unwieldy to steal the march on a virus-like insurgent, and there is a danger that its limitations arise from the core characteristics of a strategic era rather than short-term obstacles. The US – the framework provider – has the kinetic power to win global wars, but has no vision of the international structures with which to conduct a global counter-insurgency campaign. In the prevailing twentieth-century thinking, the day-to-day operations in Afghanistan and Iraq are seen as the front lines of the problem; success there is therefore also the success of the overall campaign. It follows that Washington's problem-solving energy is largely directed to what are perceived as the 'front lines' of the problem. But in the greater span of global jihad, from exclusion to activism, there are no genuine front lines, and Afghanistan and Iraq do not offer us the opportunity for genuine manoeuvre. Alas, the strategic populations and the virtual dimensions, where opportunities for manoeuvre do exist, are areas where the world's leading superpower is least inclined to exploit with any degree of conviction.

Outlined below are five proposals, which seek to alter the conditions that underwrite the Coalition and its approach in favour of achieving a more manoeuvrist counter-strategy. They also challenge the continuing acceptance of political and conceptual limitations that are in danger of becoming the characteristics of our strategic era. The sum of these efforts would be to create a cohesive and more legitimate coalition, which might share important values and have an agreed modus operandi. The benefits of greater moral and practical unity will inexorably transfer themselves into the routine tactical problems that seem to be the constant target of lessons-learned analysis. Briefly, there are five recommendations:

- Revitalize or re-forge a more cohesive alliance.
- Secure the strategic populations against subversion.
- Simplify the operational space.
- Develop a civil-military concept of operations for international counter-insurgency operations.
- Globalize (rather than state-centre) the coalition's priorities.

1. Revitalize or re-forge a more cohesive alliance

The 2002 National Security Strategy of the Unites States is often criticized by those who reject the need for countering jihad. This paper firmly argues for countering jihadist insurgents and, above all, the need to create more realistic conditions for achieving success. The 'War on Terror' manifesto and the relationship and nature of the federation of concerned states, which have pledged themselves to support it, are obstacles. The importance of morale has been disregarded. The jihadist adversary is very small but it radiates energy to its constituency with an impulsive zeal. The US manifesto, which might have provided an equivalent moral energy to the coalition, fails in this respect because it is no more than an immediate response to 9/11. Its operational scope is too wide and its cultural 'message' is too narrowly American. It fails to enlist the full-hearted support and practical energy of its potential allies. Furthermore, there is now a more developed understanding of the organic and stateless nature of the jihadist insurgency, which raises questions about campaign priorities and the absence of an agreed international approach.

A global counter-strategy against jihadist insurgency anticipates a campaign lasting more than a decade. The first requirement for its success is to create a political instrument that will last for the duration of a counter-strategy and, above all, provides the sources of inspiration for a strong alliance of contributing states. The US and its partners therefore

need a new inspiration and a new alliance whose charter should express:
- A more inspiring political vision; the articulation of the common values of members of the alliance that has the same inspirational conviction as the preamble of the United Nations Charter ('We the peoples of the United Nations…').
- A greater sense of inclusion; an alliance of states, which includes major powers, regional representatives and also has a sufficient diversity of members to convey a greater authority and legitimacy.
- A more multicultural personality; an alliance that cannot be seen to represent only the culture and interests of the Western states, in which its global and Muslim elements are represented as equal partners.
- A common counter-strategy; a standing agreement between contributor nations, which besides explaining the operational concept also determines the status of human rights, common legal procedures for dealing with captured insurgents, extradition, the presence of alliance forces stationed on members' territory, information sharing, cost sharing and government accountability.

In the prevailing climate of a Bush administration, the prospect of a new alliance on these terms is bleak. The political cost for the US and its prevailing administration is probably too high. A stronger alliance needs to include states that have famously rejected the US 'war on terror' but the price for their membership may be US policy changes on Israel and the occupation of Iraq. The concept of a multinational alliance may be uncomfortable for a US population that continues to be insular; however, in the long term these sacrifices may be the realistic cost of greater global security. At present, two things are certain: first, to succeed the current campaign will have to run beyond the operational theatres of Afghanistan and Iraq and will last for more than a decade; and second, that the current Coalition will not survive in its present form for that long.

2. Secure the Strategic Populations against Subversion

Each concerned state with a military contingent in the coalition has a scale of priorities by which to decide the emphasis of its security efforts. The spate of analysis following the London bombers in July 2005 and the more gradual efforts to define Islamic jihad both argue for an inversion of these priorities in many EU states. This reappraisal recognizes that for many concerned EU states, the strategic centre of gravity is now their own population, not the 'front lines' in Afghanistan and Iraq. Moreover, until a reconfigured alliance emerges, attrition by a massive deployment of troops and funds is the best-case scenario in the overseas theatres. A shift of analytical emphasis reveals that the engine rooms of international jihad lie in the strategic population. The security of both the Muslim minority and the mainstream population, which we have taken for granted for so long in the EU, is jeopardized. The paper argues for greater emphasis and more resources to be allocated, if necessary diverted, to *preventing* subversion rather than reacting to its consequences.

Unchallenged by state security, the Islamic recruiter is free to move and search out his targets in the Muslim community. The recruiter is also unchallenged by reality; his act of subversion takes place in an alternative world. This paper argues for a re-ordering of national priorities in a way that raises the visibility of this situation and organizes a much more determined campaign to challenge the recruiter and to introduce a stabilizing form of reality into the world of the would-be recruit. The benefit for the EU state is that against an adversary that has no vulnerable rear areas, this seems to be a critical point at which to interdict the path from subversion to activism. Interrupting the process here also confers a longer-term security on the state, the morale of its armed forces abroad and the security of the individual in the day-to-day environment of the urban area. A more determined campaign to challenge the recruiter would require:

- More Muslim role models and positive influential figures at the community level; this refers to efforts to recruit more Muslims into the police and special branch, secular teachers, as military officers, local government and local NGOs.
- Stronger Muslim institutions: the encouragement of voluntary regulation or regulation under existing laws of Muslim institutions so that influential figures leading them and working in them are accountable to the community they serve.
- A more secular emphasis on Asian culture.
- A more effective presence in the virtual dimension; this refers to the need to challenge the absence of reality in the jihadist message to mount a greater secular presence on the Muslim areas of the web. A counter-strategy needs to recognize the potential of bloggers as an instrument to challenge the metaphysical freedom of the recruiter.
- More NGOs working at the likely points of subversion; there are already Muslim NGOs at the frontlines of the campaign to challenge

subversion – they need to be encouraged to proliferate into every community with the assistance of public funding.

3. Simplify the Operational Space

In a containment operation where the adversary is less potent and the international response less committed, it is possible for the gradual efforts of an international force to return a country to a more secure environment and resuscitate civil society through a series of independently run programmes. But in a proxy war zone facing a more determined enemy, the counteracting efforts of fractious civil and military elements are disabling. Negative briefing, the prevention of information sharing and instinctive non-collaboration slows down the momentum of the campaign.

The incoherence of the international response is a core condition of the current strategic era. The military, humanitarian and development assets, often provided by the same group of donor states as part of the same response effort, are unmanageable. There are too many moving parts and, under the present circumstances, no chance of persuading them to act with a workable degree of coherence. Military forces and civil agencies tend to see themselves as individual actors but the local population and the insurgents see them as part of the same foreign intervention. Some civil agencies may feel the collective disregard for moral, political and operational cohesion is a necessary condition for maintaining their independent status, but the population and the jihadists see it as a collective lack of conviction and exploit it.

Bilateral donors who contribute towards development aid, humanitarian relief and military forces view this incoherence with a baffling indifference. Departments of the same government fund national programmes and deploy their military forces, which act against each other when they reach the operational space. The donor nation, observing this dysfunction from the perspective of its embassy makes no move to exercise an effective oversight. The weight of responsibility on donors to change this situation is growing. In a proxy war zone, the smaller proportion of freelance civil agencies, and the greater number of contractors taking their place, puts the possibility of simplifying the unnecessary chaos in the operational space squarely into the hands of donor states.

The purpose of these recommendations is to emphasize the urgency and approach needed to distinguish a proxy war zone from that of a containment operation, to reduce the number of independent actors in the operational space and to organize the remainder into functional sectors. This sets out to exclude the NGO element of the response from the operational space of an intervention, except individual elements under contract and as part of a functional sector that is subordinated to the campaign director.

- Donors to form a committee of concerned states related to a particular war zone.
- Appointment of a single campaign director, who is also the director of the committee of concerned states and donors.
- The director, the senior executive of the occupying powers until interim host government is fully established, is to:
  – control access to the war zone;
  – oversee the entire restoration and counter-insurgency campaign as a single entity;
  – orchestrate the changing priorities of the international effort as the campaign progresses; and
  – participate in strategic decision-making bodies beyond the operational space that concern the campaign.
- The creation of functional sectors; multi-mandated NGOs and commercial contractors will be subordinated into functional sectors of the response. These may include sectors for development, political regeneration, economic rebuilding and security reform. Personnel from NGOs and private commercial companies may be hired into these sectors as units and as individuals, each having an employment contract to the coalition directorate. They will be integrated into a coalition structure and not function as independent NGOs and private companies.
- Any private security companies and NGOs operating outside the integrated sectors above will have to be licensed by a global authority and authorized by the campaign directorate to gain legal access to the operational space.
- 'Strictly humanitarian actors'; a small number of international organizations will be recognized as humanitarian actors in this category. They will comprise the only body that is independent of the coalition in the operational space. They will be distinct in appearance, funding and organize their own military protection.

4. Develop a civil-military concept of operations for international counter-insurgency operations

Military doctrine is largely declassified and becoming more accessible to the public through the web. Doctrine is a crucial element of cohesion, especially in the context of international forces with a multi-sectoral civil element. Translated into procedures and training it becomes the glue which holds the otherwise disparate elements together. The absolute failure to design a common doctrine for a coalition intervention stems largely form an absence of a genuine inter-sectoral doctrine at national level (see above).

The reasons for analytical disappointment with US military doctrine[2] could also be applied to the UK Ministry of Defence efforts to conceptualize recent British experience in the same field. The UK's Joint Warfare Publications have largely failed to recognize the presence of an adversary that is implied by the concept of *containment*, and even more so by *intervention*. The 1996 version of Peace Support Operations briefly mentions 'the risk of local armed opposition'[3] before devoting itself entirely to the explanation of the civil nature of the international response. By 2004 the updated version, 'The Military Contribution to Peace Support Operations',[4] has taken the denial of an adversarial presence to new levels by completely removing any intimation that might lead a reader to suspect that these operations were opposed by armed insurgents. While the tide of academic research points to the prospect of a hugely complicated (and the need for a completely revised) counter-strategy, the UK's joint doctrine has continued to embellish civil-military procedures in a tiny sector of (apparently) unopposed peace activities in which the majority of its expeditionary forces had not been deployed for some time.[5] The situation is not saved by the UK's Army Field Manual series, whose most recent doctrine on counter-insurgency was issued directly prior to 9/11. The US Marine Corps' Small Wars 21, probably the most recently published doctrine at the time of writing, recognizes the importance of a new form of adversary,[6] the 'ultra terrorists', but suggests no genuinely new counter-strategy by which to defeat it.

To be fair, doctrine writes cannot create principles from a conceptual vacuum. An internationally acceptable concept of operations assumes agreements, alliances and shared values that in reality do not exist; in Washington and Whitehall there are different conceptual interpretations of the jihadist insurgency between departments of the same government.

Doctrine writers synthesize an evolutionary process that is already taking place, especially in British doctrine, which is a bottom-up process. The local success of intrepid pioneers later becomes the substance of mainstream thinking. In respect of complex insurgency, the next generation of pioneers are already at the front lines and there is a well-organized cycle of activity in the British and US military for capturing the lessons of tactical success for future contingents. In the UK Ministry of Defence the next step, to distil and transfer this experience to a more universal form, is about to take place. However, this process is narrowly focused on the military activities in the operational space and, perhaps in the British case, is premature. The problem facing doctrine writers on both sides of the Atlantic is whether to synthesize this limited tactical view of what is turning out to be a much wider campaign, or wait for a more inclusive concept to emerge, which might also achieve coherence and manoeuvre.

A more forward-looking concept would have to recognize:

- The organic, unstructured nature of the adversary, its global dispersal and the inspiring nature of its credo.
- The global context of the counter-strategy and the need for a more effective international civil-military alliance.
- The rethinking of the traditional levels of conflict to reflect the integration of the operational, strategic and virtual.
- That popular support is a campaign-winning condition and is won and lost in the operational, strategic and virtual dimensions.
- The paradox of the international response which, in the operational space, needs to be more coherent with simple centralized structures (as for a conventional theatre of war), but in the strategic space needs to be less formally structured and place more emphasis on community action by strongly motivated local institutions and authorities (in contrast to a theatre of war) .
- That Coalition commanders need to be able to move and act with the same agility between the operational, strategic and virtual as their opponent.

5 Globalize (rather than state-centre) the Coalition's priorities

Government officials and military staff will read the above list with disbelief, especially the recommendation to re-negotiate an international alliance to gain greater cohesion and achieve a more inspired outlook. The problem for Coalition contributors is their statehood, their position in an international system where the condition for membership is being a state. The imperatives of state collide with the requirements of alliance, particularly the necessary concessions that each member has to make and the individual subordination to the collective ethic. In this case it would be an alliance that has to act globally and intrusively. Western states are still fastened into a twentieth-century paradigm in which the constant failure of the UN is symptomatic of wider, national rejection of global versions of collective security.

The jihadist, however, is a genuinely global phenomenon. He is increasingly stateless; he flits from community to community searching for opportunities regardless of state boundaries. He survives by adaptation; he has an opposing approach to the government official. The jihadist impulse is Darwinian; as part of an organic system the individual follows a path dictated by constant and drastic change even to the point of adopting suicide bombing as a way to strike his enemies. The jihadist regards the above measures with equanimity; he would see them as manoeuvrist, understand their impact on his modus operandi and, from a stateless perspective, also understand them as feasible steps for an opponent to take. The point is that the jihadist would take these measures himself if they were required, just as surely as his state-centred opponent would not. The baggage of statehood becomes a major asset for the global insurgent. In this relationship the global virus will always move ahead of the coalition of states.

For a global counter-strategy to succeed, it requires a small revolution in the leading countries, the institutions and the departmentally-minded government officials which make up its constituent parts. This is not anticipated. However, there are degrees of change; arguing for the absolute should not be allowed to become the enemy of incremental progress. Achieving a more authoritative, more representative, more multicultural alliance by degrees is a reasonable price for a more secure and therefore more humane environment in the longer term.

Notes

Introduction

[1] Joint Doctrine and Concepts Centre, UK Ministry of Defence, *British Defence Doctrine*, DSDC(L) Llanelli, 2001, p. 3.5.

[2] Joint Doctrine and Concepts Centre, UK Ministry of Defence, *British Defence Doctrine*, DSDC(L) Llanelli, 1996, pp. 4.8 and 4.9.

[3] *Ibid.* pp. 4.10 and 4.11.

[4] This is explained in British doctrine as the 'OODA loop', referring a decision-making cycle of actions Observation-Orientation-Decision-Action-Observation. UK Ministry of Defence, 2001, *op cit.* p. 3.6.

Chapter 1

[1] For example, in 1989 UNAVEM 1 to Angola, UNTAG to Namibia, ONUCA to Central America. Blue Helmets, Parts V and VI.

[2] Birger Heldt and Peter Wallensteen, *Peacekeeping Operations: Global Patterns of Intervention and Success, 1948-2004* (Folk Bernadotte Academy Publications, 2005), p. 19.

[3] The term was accepted into wider use after the 1994 IASC conference working paper, and redefined recently in IASC Reference Paper 28, June 2004. The UK Ministry of Defence accepts the IASC definition. See MoD Pamphlet (CIMIC), p. 3.90.

[4] These conditions were humanitarian suffering on an enormous scale, a civil war involving several armed factions, the collapse of state infrastructure, an absence of governance, fragile individual security, large numbers of displaced civilians, refugees and unchallenged criminal activities and the likelihood of ethnic cleansing and genocide. See UK Ministry of Defence, *Peace Support Operations*, 1996, Chapter 2.

[5] Typically, the area of operations would be imprecisely defined. It might lie astride several international borders, without front lines and with only a rash of incidents to indicate the critical area.

[6] This refers to the UN forces that deployed to Central America, Namibia, Cambodia, Mozambique, Somalia and Croatia. See *Blue Helmets*, Chapters 5-8.

[7] UN Doc. S/110521Rev. 27 Oct 1973. This gives a complete list of the essential preconditions for successful traditional peacekeeping forces.

[8] This was reflected in the configuration of forces, the increased use of armoured vehicles and the gradually altering doctrines for their use.

[9] Jarat Chopra, John Mackinlay and Larry Minear, *Report on the Cambodian Peace Process*, Research Report 165 (Oslo: Norwegian Institute of International Affairs, 1993), p. 9. The concerned states at Paris suffered from negotiators' double vision; their version of the Khmer Rouge co-operation versus the intelligence communities' widely circulated forecast of the KR's certain opposition.

[10] See Jock Covey, Michael Dziedzic and Leonard Hawley (eds.), *The Quest for Viable Peace* (New York: US Institute of Peace, 2005), Chapter 3.
[11] Entry phase, Stabilization phase and Garrison phase.
[12] This refers primarily to countries such as Afghanistan, Somalia, North-West Frontier Province of Pakistan and Yemen, but it could also describe any area where the environment was so dangerous as to discourage any form of international regulation or policing without military support. By the same token, these areas encouraged and attracted all forms of piracy, kidnap, hijack and trafficking, and acted as a refuge for globally organized activism.
[13] *9/11 Commission Report*, Chapter 4.
[14] For example, it took almost twenty years for the members of the NATO Alliance to develop a workable structure for political oversight and international command in order to direct a defensive campaign in a series of very closely defined strips of territory between themselves and the Warsaw pact forces.
[15] At the time of writing, this manifests itself more as a general awareness of the importance of skills and procedures that were learned in the Cold War period. There is also the publication of the UK Ministry of Defence, 'Tactical Handbook for Operations Other than War'. D/DGD&D/18/34/83/, January 2000.
[16] Designed by Niklas Plank.
[17] UK Ministry of Defence (JWP), 1996, *op cit.*, pp. 1.9 and 1.10.
[18] This is based on my own involvement in complex emergency teaching at staff colleges and officer training courses in the UK and NATO.
[19] UK Ministry of Defence, *The Military Contribution to Peace Support Operations*, (JWP 3-50), Llanelli, 2004, pp. 2-14.
[20] For example, during the initial phase of the intervention on the ground in Afghanistan (2002), it was possible for General Franks and his staff at CENTCOM in Tampa, Florida to monitor progress in minute detail via systems moving with the soldiers at the leading edge of the advance.
[21] UK Ministry of Defence, *British Defence Doctrine*, 2001, *op cit.*, p. 1.4.
[22] UK Ministry of Defence, 2004, *op cit.*, pp. 2.14 and 2.15.
[23] For example, in the containment operations of the 1990s, the 'operational space' in Liberia and Kosovo included ports, air fields, approach roads and displaced populations which lay in adjacent states.
[24] As defined by the Inter-Agency Standing Committee, 28 June 2004, 'Civil-Military Relationships in Complex Emergencies', http://ochaonline.un.org/mcdu/guidelines
[25] See list and analysis in John Mackinlay, 'Co-operating in the Conflict Zone', *NATO Fellowship Paper*, NATO website, August 2002, Part 1, 'Defining the Conflict Zone', pp. 6-18.
[26] This refers to the response cells set up by ministries of foreign affairs to deploy an effective diplomatic presence as well as an office for the co-ordination of national programmes swiftly into the operational space. RUSI Conference 14-15 July 2005, 'Transformation of Military Operations on the Cusps', Session 3, submission by UK Foreign and Commonwealth Office.
[27] UK Ministry of Defence, 2004, *op cit.*, Annex B, 'Understanding Key Non-Governmental and International Organisations', Paragraph B 13.
[28] A 'proxy war' zone refers, in this case, to the wider struggle between the US and its Coalition partners against global jihad. 'Global War Against Terror' is not a primary concern for the majority of Afghans and Iraqis; nevertheless, Iraq and Afghanistan have become conflict areas recognized by both sides where this struggle takes place.
[29] The system for news distribution has been described as directly comparable to the internet. An excellent description of a parallel network in its simplest form is in Ned Snell, *Sams Teach Yourself the Internet in 24 Hours*, 'Hour 1, What is the Internet?', (Indiana: SAMS, 1999).
[30] The substance of the relevant presentation is embargoed. See conference synopsis: Royal United Services Institute and US Joint Forces Command, 'Transformation of Operations on the

Notes

Cusps', *op cit.*, 14-15 March 2005.

[31] In the UK, for example, local councils are unable or reluctant to categorize and therefore assess the numerical size of their constituent populations by their ethnicity.

[32] The ease of assimilation varies with the opportunity for immigrants to find rewarding employment, racial hostility and the degree to which they have managed to establish themselves as a community. A well-organized minority that has been established for some time will have its own internal structures for welfare and leadership. It therefore caters for legally and illegally immigrated arrivals with greater success. Assimilation is also influenced by the distance to their own country of origin. In France, immigrant Algerians can visit Algeria on a regular basis by car ferry from the EU's Mediterranean ports; in the UK, however, visiting 'home' for a Pakistani requires a much greater effort in terms of time and expense. The incentive to accommodate to local conditions in the latter case may therefore be greater. Interview with Alison Pargiter, 26 July 2005. Alison Pargiter, *North African Immigrants in Europe and Political Violence* (to be published in 2006).

[33] UK Ministry of Defence (JWP), 1996, *op cit.*, pp. 4.7 and 4.8.

[34] See David Rhode, 'GI's in Afghanistan on Hunt , but Now for Hearts and Minds', *The New York Times*, 30 March 2004.

[35] IASC 2004, *op cit.*, paragraph 46.

[36] IASC 2004, *op cit.*, paragraph 17.

[37] See Hugo Slim, 'With or Against, Humanitarian Agencies and Coalition Counter Insurgency', Centre for Humanitarian Dialogue, Geneva 2004.

Chapter 2

[1] John Arquilla, David Ronfeldt and Michele Zanini, 'Networks, Netwar and Information-Age Terrorism', in Ian Lesser *et al.*, *Countering New Terrorism*, (Santa Monica: RAND, 1999).

[2] John Arquilla and David Ronfeldt (eds), *Networks and Netwars: The Future of Terror, Crime and Militancy*, (Santa Monica: RAND, 2001).

[3] *Ibid.*, Chapter 1, p. 5.

[4] *Ibid.*, p. 15.

[5] This issue is addressed in Chapter Three.

[6] David Kilcullen, 'Countering Global Insurgency', unpublished paper, Washington and Canberra, November 2004.

[7] See for example collection by Lawrence Freedman, Superterrorism Policy Responses (Blackwell, 2002) and W. Bowen and A. Stewart (eds), *Terrorism in the UK*, SCSI Occasional Paper No. 50 (Shrivenham Wilts: JDCC, 2005), in which the majority of papers refer to insurgency as defined by Kilcullen and others as 'terrorism'.

[8] UK Ministry of Defence, 'Counter Insurgency Operations', *Army Field Manual*, Vol. 1 Part 10, Published by DG&D, 2001.

[9] Kilcullen, *op cit.*, p. 8.

[10] *Ibid.*, p. 35.

[11] Richard Brennan, Adam Grissom, Sara Daly, Peter Chalk, William Rosenau, K. Sepp and Stephen Dalzell, *Future Insurgency Threats*, RAND, February 2005.

[12] Although Hoffman and Kilcullen also work for RAND, individuals in RAND and outside analysts agree that the conclusions of each study represented an independently argued case.

[13] US Department of State, *Patterns of Global Terrorism*, (Washington , DC: US Department of State, April 2003), p. xiii. The title is derived from Title 22 of the United States Code, section 2656f (d).

[14] Brennan *et al.* (2005) *op cit.* p. xii.

[15] *Ibid.*, p. xiv.

[16] *Ibid.*, p. 166.
[17] Hoffman, *op cit.*, p. 17.
[18] Following reports that a 'third Islamist terror cell is planning multiple suicide bomb attacks against tube trains'. See Don Van Natta Jr., 'Britain goes on High Alert', *The New York Times*, 5 August , 2005.
[19] Broadcast on satellite channel threatened further attacks in London and the US. *The New York Times*, *op cit.*
[20] The US military spokesman's assessment of increased offensive bombing. See *The New York Times*, *op cit.*
[21] Daniel McGrory and Sean O' Neill, 'Inside the hunt for the London bombers', *The Times*, 6 August 2005, p. 11.
[22] Roya Nikkah and Tariq Tahir, 'He cut off all contact with us, says bombers's family', *Sunday Telegraph*, 17 July 2005.
[23] *The Independent On Sunday*, 31 July 2005 (see box on page 7).
[24] The New York Times, *op cit.*
[25] Jonathan Raban, 'Jihad on the High Street', *The Independent on Sunday*, 31 July 2005, p. 29.
[26] Gilles Kepel, *The War for Muslim Minds*, (Cambridge, Massachusetts: Havard University Press, 2004), pp. 95–97.
[27] BBC News, 23 December 2004, 'Madrid bomb commission ends probe', http//news.bbc.co.uk/1/hi/world/europe/
[28] Hugo Slim, 'Violent Beliefs', *RUSI Journal* (Vol. 150 No. 2, April 2005), pp. 20–23.
[29] *Ibid*
[30] *Ibid.*
[31] '90 minutes from murder', *The Observer*, 17 July 2005, front page.
[32] Kepel, *op cit.*, pp. 190–191.
[33] A. Norfolk, 'Extremists preyed on brother's feeling of isolation', *The Times*, 6 August 2003, p. 10.
[34] Kepel, *op cit.*, p. 252.
[35] Both rebel-held areas have been the subject of a number of films featured on the main TV channels.
[36] Kilcullen, *op cit.*, p. 26.
[37] Olivier Roy, *Globalised Islam: The Search for a New 'Ummah'*, (London: Hurst, 2004), pp. 268–269.
[38] Kilcullen, *op cit.*, p. 9.
[39] Jason Burke, *Al-Qaeda Casting a Shadow of Terror*, (London: I.B. Tauris, 2003).
[40] UK Ministry of Defence (DGD&D), 'Counter Insurgency Operations', *Army Field Manual*, Vol. 1 Part 10, p. A.1.1, paragraph 1. (London: MoD, July 2001)
[41] Jonathan Stevenson, 'Pragmatic Counter-Terrorism', *Survival* Vol. 43 No. 4, Winter 2001-02, p. 35.
[42] From Zawahiri's text, 'Knights under the Prophets Banner', cited in Kepel, *op cit.*, p. 95.
[43] RAND, *op cit.*, pp. 7-20.

Chapter 3

[1] UN Report of Security in Iraq Accountability Panel (SIAP), New York, 3 March 2004.
[2] Chaloka Beyani, 'The "Global War on Terror": issues and trends in the use of force and humanitarian law', ODI, Humanitarian Policy Group Briefing, No. 10, July 2003.
[3] In Afghanistan, it is the United Nations Assistance Mission in Afghanistan established by UN Security Council Res/1401, 28 March 2002, www.unama-afg.org
[4] Interview with Victoria Wheeler, Humanitarian Policy Group, Overseas Development

Notes

Institute. London, 12 August 2005.

[5] Colonel Christopher Meyer, US Army Reserve (PSC co-ordination staff Baghdad), interviewed at Kingston, Ontario, March 2005.

[6] In post-Dayton Bosnia, General Mike Jackson, as Commander of the British sector, also participated in radio and TV shows in addition to news interviews.

[7] In Thompson's accounts and in security forces terminology, the insurgents in Malaya were generally referred to as the CT (Communist Terrorists), which recognized the acts of terror they had committed but did not detract from the general understanding that they were part of an insurgency.

[8] UK Ministry of Defence (2001), 'Counter Insurgency', *op cit.*, Chapter 2.

[9] See Zawahiri's manifesto cited in Kepel, *op cit.*, p. 95.

[10] Antonio Donini, 'Afghanistan; Peace is Jobs and Security', presentation at NGO-Military contact group research seminar, Royal College of Defence Studies, London, 8 April 2005.

[11] Kepel, *op cit.*, pp. 292-293.

[12] This is described in British doctrine as the insurgents' centre of strategic gravity. (*Ibid.*)

[13] Unpublished trip report for the US Department of Defense, Washington, D.C., June 2005.

[14] Hillier

[15] '...the NGOs, who are such a force multiplier for us such an important part of our combat team', Colin Powell addressing NGO Leaders, 26 October 2001. Cites in Hugo Slim, *op cit.* (Geneva, 2004)

[16] UK Ministry of Defence (JDCC), 'Civil-Military Co-operation', Interim Joint Warfare Publication 3-90, DSDC(L), Llanelli, November 2003.

[17] According to lists of 'martyrs' reflected on Islamist websites, the suicide bombers of Iraq are an internationalist brigade of Arabs, with more than half coming from Saudi Arabia and a significant minority from other countries on Iraq's borders, such as Syria and Kuwait. Susan Glasser, '"Martyrs" in Iraq Mostly Saudis: Websites Track Suicide Bombings', *Washington Post*, 15 May 2005.

[18] The political negotiations in Northern Ireland and the manifesto in Malaya show that British campaign directors seldom seemed to have many problems about this as long as the end state was still favourable to long-term interests. It is not clear whether US policy-makers share this relaxed attitude.

[19] Roy, *op cit.*, pp. 308–309.

[20] Kepel, *op cit.*, pp. 250–251.

[21] For example, the Lucman Institute and Forward Thinking are two local NGOs who work to help isolated Muslims in the minority communities of UK.

Chapter 4

[1] *Ibid.*, p. xxiii.

[2] UK MOD(JWP), 1996, *op cit.*, pages 2-2

[3] UK MOD(JWP) 2004, *op cit.*

[4] See chart on page; the majority of UK forces were by this time deployed to intervention forces in a proxy war zone where they were very much opposed, besides being less international in scope, than the UN containment operations which are largely featured in the JWP series referenced.

[5] See Marine Corps Combat Development Command 2005, *Small Wars 21st Century*, Quantico VA, Chapter 2 'What's New about Small Wars?'